Pennsylvania Dutch Recipes

1st Printing 1999

420 Weaver Road
Millersburg, PA 17061

Printed in U.S.A.

I.S.B.N. 0-9670627-1-3

Front cover by Bill Klouser.

DEDICATION

We dedicate this book to our Mothers and Grandmothers, for teaching us the joy of baking and cooking.

"To Our Mothers and Grandmothers"

Your head has rocked the cradle
For little ones so dear.
You soothed their fretful heartaches,
You dried their falling tear.
You've been a nurse and teacher,
A secretary, too.
You cooked and washed and mended;
There was so much to do!
You laid a firm foundation
Through every passing day;
You taught God's word so steadfast,
And told us how to pray.
You emphasized the virtues
Of faith and charity,
Of walking close to Jesus
In deep humility!
The passing years are fleeting
Gray hairs adorn your brow.
Life's sun is traveling westward,
Its rays are fainter now!
The pathway worn and weary
With trails will be past;
And in a home eternal
There'll be sweet rest at last!

HOW TO PRESERVE A HUSBAND

Be careful in your selection. Do not choose too young and take only such varieties that have been reared in a good moral and Christian atmosphere. When once decided upon and settled, let that part remain forever settled and give your entire thought to further use.

Some insist on keeping them in a pickle, while others are constantly getting them in hot water.

Even poor varieties may be made sweet, tender and good by garnishing them with patience, well sweetened with smiles, and flavored with kisses to taste; then wrap them well in a mantel of charity, kept warm with a steady fire of domestic devotion, and serve with peaches and cream. When thus prepared, they will keep for years.

Appetizers Relishes & Pickles

We become noble persons when we are willing to listen and to investigate before making a decision.

The road to the heart of the average man
Is by the way of the stomach, I ween
And there is nothing like pickles to sharpen the edge
Of the masculine appetite keen.

One of the quaintest bits of hospitality of the Pennsylvania Dutch is the celebrated custom known as the "Seven Sweets and the Seven Sours."

Tradition has it that the housewife must set the table with precisely seven sweets and seven sours. Those famous sweets and sours usually consist of various forms of preserves and pickles - all home made.

Sweet pickles will balance sour pickles and pickled eggs and red beets will check with ginger tomatoes. Strawberry jam, or spiced peaches, apple butter, chow-chow, mustard pickles, pickled cabbage, pickled pears are among the many items which can be chosen from the long list of sweets and sours by the housewife.

The following pages contain some real
Pennsylvania Dutch recipes.

APPETIZERS, RELISHES & PICKLES

APPETIZER MEATBALLS

2 lb. ground beef
1 lb. bulk pork sausage
1 (5 oz.) can evaporated milk
2 c. old fashioned oats
½ tsp. pepper
2 tsp. chili powder
½ tsp. garlic powder
2 ½ tsp. salt
2 eggs
½ c. chopped onion

Sauce (If you like sauce, double this recipe):

2 c. catsup
1 ½ c. brown sugar
½ tsp. garlic powder
½ c. chopped onion

Mix all meatball ingredients together. Shape into 1-inch balls. Place in baking pan. Combine sauce ingredients and pour over meatballs. Bake at 350° for 1 hour.

Mary Ann Smucker

PARTY MIX

4 c. Cheerios
4 c. Corn Chex
4 c. Rice Chex
4 c. Wheat Chex
pretzels, peanuts and Cheez-Its as desired
½ lb. butter
2 Tbsp. Worcestershire sauce
2 tsp. celery salt
2 tsp. seasoned salt

Melt the butter and stir in the Worcestershire sauce, celery salt and seasoned salt. Pour over party mix. Bake in 250° oven for 1 hour. Stir every 15 minutes.

Anna King

PARTY MIX

1 box Rice Chex
1 box Wheat Chex
1 box Cheerios
1 box cheese crackers
1 lb. nuts
1 lb. pretzel sticks
5 sticks butter
2 Tbsp. onion salt
2 Tbsp. Accent
1 Tbsp. Worcestershire sauce
1 ½ Tbsp. garlic salt

Mix all dry ingredients. Melt butter and add seasonings. Pour over dry ingredients. Place in 225° oven and bake for 2 hours, stirring every ½ hour.

Fannie Riehl

FANNIE'S SNACK CRACKERS

1 c. vegetable oil
1 Tbsp. dill weed seed
½ tsp. garlic powder
1 pkg. Hidden Valley Ranch mix

Pour mix over 2 (12 ounce) packages little oyster crackers. Let set 1 hour.

Susie King

CRACKER DIP

2 (8 oz.) soft cream cheese
2 (8 oz.) sour cream
1 ½ c. granulated sugar
1 tsp. vinegar
pinch of salt
1 pkg. Hidden Valley Ranch mix

Mix well.

Susie S. King

CHEESE DIP

2 eggs, beaten
2 Tbsp. sugar
2 Tbsp. vinegar
pinch of salt
lump butter
8 oz. cream cheese
1 small onion
1 green pepper

Thicken the eggs, sugar, vinegar, pinch of salt and lump of butter on low heat. When cool add remaining ingredients.

Naomi King

VEGETABLE DIP

8 oz. sour cream
8 oz. mayonnaise
1 pkg. Ranch style salad mix

Mix together and store in refrigerator until needed.

Helen Miller

CHEESE BALL

2 (8 oz.) pkg. cream cheese
8 oz. Cracker Barrel sharp Cheddar cheese, softened
1 Tbsp. green pepper, chopped
1 Tbsp. onion, chopped
2 Tbsp. Worcestershire sauce
1 tsp. lemon juice
dash of salt

Mix together well and shape in ball. Chill.

Naomi Grace Zook

DIP (HOT)

8 oz. jar Cheez Whiz
11 ½ oz. can condensed bean with bacon soup

Combine ingredients, heat and serve with corn chips. Hot and hearty!

Sara Stoltzfoos

CHIP AND DIP

2 eggs
2 Tbsp. sugar
2 Tbsp. vinegar
salt
lump of butter
8 oz. cream cheese
onions and peppers to taste, chopped fine

Beat eggs. Add sugar, vinegar, salt and butter. Thicken on low heat. When cool, add the cream cheese, onions and peppers.

Anna King

CHOW CHOW

9 c. sugar
4 c. vinegar
8 c. water
2 tsp. salt
1 to 2 tsp. celery salt

Heat brine until boiling. Mix vegetables: string beans, kidney, soy, limas, lots of carrots, corn, peas, pickles, cauliflower, watermelon rind, a bit of onions and peppers. All vegetables must be cooked except onions and peppers. Drain juice off. Pack in jars and fill with brine. This brine may be used to can string beans, sugar peas, etc.

Sara Stoltzfus

PICKLE RELISH

4 qt. pickles
1 qt. onions
½ qt. peppers
3 tsp. salt
2 tsp. mustard seed
1 tsp. turmeric
2 tsp. celery seed
2 lb. sugar
2 c. vinegar

Grind pickles, onions and peppers. Put salt on and let stand 3 hours, then drain. Cook everything and simmer 3 minutes. Put in jars and seal. Makes 9 pints.

Liz Stoltzfus

SWEET PEPPER RELISH

2 oz. celery seed
1 doz. red sweet peppers
1 doz. green sweet peppers
1 doz. onions

Grind in food chopper. Soak for 10 minutes in boiling water, then drain. Put the following into a kettle over heat.

1 ½ pt. vinegar
2 lb. brown sugar
3 Tbsp. salt
½ tsp. pepper
1 tsp. cinnamon
2 Tbsp. mustard seed

Add peppers, onions and celery seed. Boil for about 10 to 15 minutes, then jar and seal.

Linda Fisher

PICKLE RELISH

8 c. cucumbers, cut up into small pieces
1 big onion, cut up into small pieces
1 stalk celery, cut up into small pieces
1 c. vinegar
3 c. sugar
2 tsp. prepared mustard
¼ tsp. pepper
2 Tbsp. salt

Heat to boiling, then put in jars.

Rachel Esh

SWEET PICKLE RELISH

4 c. coarse ground cucumber
2 Tbsp. salt
3 peppers
7 onions
3 c. sugar
6 c. vinegar
1 Tbsp. pickling spice

Combine cucumbers and salt and let stand for 1 hour. Drain and add peppers and onions. Cook for 5 minutes in sugar and vinegar mixture. Put pickling spice in bag. Put into jars and seal. Makes about 6 pints.

Sylvia Petersheim
Elizabeth Stoltzfus

SWEET PICKLE RELISH

4 qt. coarse ground pickles
2 Tbsp. salt
3 peppers (I use red ones)
7 onions
2 tsp. turmeric
5 c. sugar
6 c. vinegar
1 Tbsp. pickling spice in bag while cooking

Combine the pickles and salt and let set for 1 hour. Drain. Grind fine the peppers and onions and add to pickle and salt mixture. Add the remaining ingredients and cook 5 minutes. Can and seal.

Barbara King

BANANA PICKLES

2 c. vinegar
1 c. water
3 c. sugar
1 tsp. salt
1 tsp. celery seed
1 tsp. mustard seed
1 tsp. turmeric (if desired; makes more color)

Bring to a boil, then pour over long thinly sliced pickles. Cold pack 15 minutes in jar.

Mrs. Elam Z. Stoltzfus
Priscilla Fisher
Sara Stoltzfus
Liz Stoltzfus

MUSTARD PICKLES

1 qt. vinegar to 3 qt. water
½ c. ground mustard
1 Tbsp. saccharin
½ c. whole allspice
1 tsp. alum
½ c. salt

Makes 4 quarts.

Fannie Glick

SWEET SOUR DILL PICKLES

medium size cucumbers
onion slices
2 celery stalks, quartered
8 heads fresh dill
4 c. sugar
½ c. salt
1 qt. vinegar
2 c. water

Wash freshly picked cucumbers and cut in 1-inch chunks or in quarters enough to fill 4 quart jars. To each jar, add 3 or 4 slices onion, 2 pieces celery and 2 heads dill. Dissolve sugar and salt in water and vinegar. Bring to a boil. Pour while hot over cucumbers in each jar to cover. Seal at once. Store in cool place. For best flavor, do not use for 30 days.

Sara Stoltzfoos

BREAD AND BUTTER PICKLES

1 gal. thin sliced pickles
2 c. sliced onions
¼ c. salt
4 ½ c. sugar
1 tsp. turmeric
2 Tbsp. mustard seed
2 c. vinegar
a little water

Slice pickles. Add onions and salt. Mix well and let stand 3 hours. Drain dry. Make juice and bring to a boil. Add pickles and bring to a good boil. Put in jars and seal.

Liz Stoltzfus
Naomi King

SACCHARIN PICKLES

2 c. water
2 c. vinegar
2 Tbsp. salt
2 Tbsp. sugar

Bring to a boil. Add ¼ teaspoon saccharin. Pack in jars and boil for 3 to 5 minutes. Makes 2 quarts.

Naomi Grace Zook

SWEET DILL PICKLES (CANNING)

2 c. water
2 c. vinegar
3 c. sugar
2 Tbsp. salt
dill
slice onion
slice garlic bulb

Heat the water, vinegar, sugar and salt to a boil. Wash and slice pickles. In each quart put 1 teaspoon dill, slice of onion and a slice of garlic bulb. Cold pack for 5 minutes.

Mrs. Edna B. Zook

SWEET DILL PICKLES

2 c. vinegar
2 c. water
3 c. sugar
2 Tbsp. salt
¼ tsp. dill seed

I also add turmeric.

Cold pack 5 minutes after they come to a hard boil. This should be enough liquid for 8 pints. Slice pickles thin and put in jars. Put onions and some dill on top of each can. Heat and pour over pickles.

Fannie Glick

BREAD AND BUTTER PICKLES

8 c. sliced cucumbers
2 c. sliced onions
2 Tbsp. salt
3 c. white sugar
2 c. white vinegar
2 tsp. celery seed
2 sticks cinnamon
4 peppers

Mix the cucumbers and onions and add the salt. Cover with water and let stand 2 hours. Combine the sugar, vinegar, celery seed, cinnamon and peppers and boil for 20 minutes, then pour over cucumbers and onions (after they're drained). Bring to a boil. Jar and seal.

Fannie Glick

BREAD AND BUTTER PICKLES

1 gal. cucumbers
8 small onions
2 green peppers
½ c. salt
sweet crisp fresh cucumbers

Wash cucumbers. Peel and slice thin. Slice onions. Chop peppers fine. Mix salt with vegetables and cover with weight. Let stand 3 hours. Drain off and make a syrup.

Syrup:

1 ½ tsp. turmeric
½ tsp. ground cloves
2 Tbsp. mustard seed
1 tsp. celery seed
2 c. vinegar
2 c. water
4 c. sugar

Mrs. Elam Z. Stoltzfus

DILL PICKLES

pickles
½ tsp. dill seed
½ tsp. minced garlic

Fill jars with pickles and add the dill seed and minced garlic.

Juice:

½ c. salt
8 c. water
2 ½ c. vinegar

For a crisp pickle, process only until water boils and remove jars.

Naomi Petersheim

KOSHER DILL PICKLES

½ tsp. alum
¼ tsp. salt
1 Tbsp. kosher dill pickle mix

Put on top of each quart packed with pickles.

8 c. water
4 c. vinegar
2 c. sugar

Cook syrup and pour over pickles. Cold pack to boiling point.

Aarianne Petersheim

CHUNK PICKLES

1 gal. pickles, cut in chunks
½ c. salt

Add salt to the pickles. Cover with boiling water and soak overnight.

2 c. each sugar, water and vinegar
1 tsp. each allspice, dry mustard, mustard seed and celery seed
½ tsp. each turmeric and alum

Boil together. Add pickles and boil again. Pack into jars and seal.

Aarianne Petersheim

7 DAY PICKLES

7 lb. cucumbers
1 qt. vinegar
8 c. sugar
2 Tbsp. salt
2 Tbsp. mixed pickle spices

Cover pickles with boiling water and let stand 24 hours. Drain and repeat 3 times using fresh water each day.

On the fifth day, cut pickles in ¼-inch slices. Combine sugar, vinegar, salt and spices and bring to a boil. Pour over sliced pickles. Let stand 24 hours.

On the sixth day, drain syrup again and bring to a boil. Pour over pickles.

On the seventh day, drain again and bring to boil. Add pickles and bring to boiling point. Pack in jars and seal.

Rachel Esh
Susie King

SWEET AND SOUR DILL PICKLES

medium size pickles
8 heads fresh dill or 1 tsp. seed
4 c. sugar
2 c. water
1 qt. vinegar
½ c. salt

Cut cucumbers in quarters or lengthwise to fill 4 quart jars. To each jar add 3 or 4 slices onions, 2 pieces of celery and 2 heads dill. Dissolve sugar and salt in vinegar and water. Bring to a boil. Pour over pickles while still hot. Cold pack 10 minutes.

Barbara King

ANNIE'S PICKLES

8 c. sliced pickles
2 onions, cut up
2 Tbsp. salt

Soak in cold water for 3 hours. Pack in jars.

Syrup:

2 c. sugar
2 tsp. celery salt
2 tsp. dry mustard
2 scant tsp. turmeric
2 tsp. salt
1 c. water
1 c. vinegar

Bring syrup to a boil. Pour over pickles in jars and cold pack 5 minutes.

Linda Fisher

RED CINNAMON PICKLES

Part One:

15 large cucumbers
2 c. pickling lime
8 ½ qt. water

Peel and cut into ½-inch slices. Scrape out center (seeds). Put rings in lime water. Let stand 24 hours. Stir occasionally as lime settles. Drain and rinse until clear. Cover with cold water. Let stand 3 hours. Drain.

Part Two:

1 c. vinegar
1 tsp. alum
½ oz. red food coloring

Place rings in pan and cover with mixture adding enough water to cover. Heat and simmer 2 hours. Drain.

Part Three:

2 c. vinegar
2 c. water
10 c. sugar
12 oz. cinnamon hearts
2 cinnamon sticks

Mix and bring to a boil. Pour over rings and cover tightly. Let set overnight. Drain and reheat syrup the next morning. The third morning, heat syrup and rings to a boil. Pack in jars.

Mary Ann Smucker

GARLIC AND DILL PICKLES

4 c. sugar
3 c. vinegar
3 c. water
3 Tbsp. salt
2 Tbsp. dill seed

Heat to dissolve sugar. Pack pickles in jars. Put 1 garlic clove and 1 bay leaf in each jar. Bring to a boil. Turn off stove. Let set in water for a few minutes.

Sylvia Stoltzfus

PICKLED CAULIFLOWER

2 large heads cauliflower
1 bunch celery

Boil both until tender and pack in 7 pint jars.

2 c. sugar
2 c. vinegar
2 c. water
2 Tbsp. salt
2 tsp. celery seed
2 tsp. mustard seed

Bring this to a boil and pour over cauliflower. Cold pack 5 minutes.

Barbara King

PICKLED CAULIFLOWER AND CARROTS

Cook desired amounts of vegetables and mix after being cooled. Pack into jars and add syrup.

Syrup Mixture:

4 c. sugar
1 Tbsp. salt
2 ½ c. water
2 c. vinegar

Cook until sugar is dissolved. Cold pack 10 minutes. A slice of hot pepper can be added to each jar to give them a "hot" flavor.

Nancy Ann Esch

PICKLED ONION RINGS

8 c. sliced onions (about 3 lb.)
boiling water
1 c. white vinegar
1 c. sugar
2 tsp. canning salt
½ tsp. mustard seed

Blanch onions in boiling water for 4 minutes. Drain. In a large saucepan, combine vinegar, sugar, salt and mustard seed. Bring to a boil. Add onions and simmer for 4 minutes. Pack into sterilized standard canning jars. Fill to ½-inch of top, making sure vinegar covers onions. Adjust lids. Process in a boiling water bath for 5 minutes. Makes 2 to 3 pints. Serve in sandwiches, on relish trays or with roast meat or game.

Rebecca K. Stoltzfus

421792

SWEET PICKLES

30 cucumbers (4-inches long and fairly thin
1 qt. vinegar
1 qt. water
16 c. sugar
1/4 c. mixed spices
1/4 c. salt

Place washed cucumbers in a crock or stainless pail or dish. Cover with freshly boiling water. Let stand 24 hours. Drain and again cover with boiling water. Continue until they have 4 hot water baths.

The fifth day, drain, rinse and slice cucumbers into 1/4-inch slices. Combine vinegar, sugar, salt and spices tied in a bag and bring to a boil. Pour over slices. Let stand 24 hours. Pour off syrup. Reheat to boiling and pour over again. Repeat 2 more days.

The ninth day, drain and reheat syrup. Pack slices in jars and cover with hot syrup. Seal at once. Makes approximately 8 pints.

Ruth Stoltzfus

Red Pepper Remedies

My grandfather often prepared a Musterole-type rub by incorporating about a tablespoonful each of powdered pepper and mustard and a little of ginger and cloves in lard, chicken, or mutton fat. A cold or ache or sprain called for a none-too-gentle massage with this hot ointment and then a hot, wet towel, on top of which went the hot water bottle.

A good ant repellent: Equal parts of borax and powdered red pepper.

Powdered red pepper is a good "warming powder" for ice skaters, walkers and policemen in winter. Dilute 1 part in 8 or 10 parts of talc and put into the shoes. Try it.

You can prevent your playful puppy from chewing up your house with a pepper treatment. Spray his favorite spots with a little water and put on a tiny bit of red (cayenne) pepper. That'll teach him.

Soups, Salads & Sauces

Praise Ye

As the earth drinks rain
After parching days
And responds to the sun's
Beneficent rays
So does a child
Blossom forth under praise.

Radish

Omit radishes from your salad if your digestion is weak: otherwise, serve them whole in salad. Do not cut them since by the time they are consumed in their cut state, they may have lost most of their nutrients by oxidation.

Eat the tops as well. When young, the greens may be included with other salad ingredients. The older greens may be steamed alone or with other vegetables. When steamed, the prickles on the older, larger leaves soften and are not noticed.

Cheerful cooks make every dish a feast.

SOUPS, SALADS & SAUCES

A RECIPE TO LIVE BY

Blend one cup of love and half cup of kindness. Add alternately in small portions, one cup of appreciation and three cups of pleasant companionship, into which has been sifted three teaspoons of deserving praise. Flavor with one teaspoon carefully chosen advise. Fold in one cup of cheerfulness to which has been added a pinch of sorrow. Pour with tender care into small clean hearts and bake until well matured. Turn out the surface of society, humbly invoke God's blessings and it will serve all mankind.

Susie King

CANNED SLEEP

½ doz. naps
40 winks
½ c. energy

Mix together and put in pints. Fill it up with water. Cook for 10 minutes. Best when served Monday morning right out of the cans. Good luck!

Susie King

TOMATO SOUP

1 peck ripe tomatoes
6 medium size onions
1 bunch celery
4 large green peppers

Cut onions, tomatoes, pepper and celery. Boil until soft. Add 1 teaspoon red pepper. Strain through a food mill. Add to liquid:

1 c. sugar
1 Tbsp. salt
½ c. melted butter
½ c. flour

Mix the melted butter and flour in a separate bowl, then add to liquid. Boil for 15 to 20 minutes. Jar while hot.

Anna Fisher

POTATO SOUP

5 or 6 medium size potatoes
1 medium size onion
2 tsp. salt
3 tsp. butter
4 c. milk
½ tsp. pepper
4 hard-boiled eggs

Cook potatoes and onions in boiling water until soft. Add milk and seasoning. Chop up the eggs.

Anna King

POTATO BROCCOLI SOUP

1 c. chopped broccoli
4 c. diced potatoes
3 eggs
¼ c. chicken broth or 1 can cream of chicken soup
2 c. milk

Add water to broccoli and potatoes. Bring to a boil. Add raw eggs and cook until vegetables are soft. Use potato masher and mash slightly. Add chicken mix and stir. Add milk and heat slowly.

Susie S. King

CREAM OF BROCCOLI AND CHEESE SOUP

2 c. chopped celery
1 c. chopped onion
1 pkg. chopped broccoli (10 oz. frozen or fresh)
1 c. cottage cheese
2 c. milk
1 can cream of chicken soup, undiluted
½ tsp. salt
⅛ tsp. pepper

Cook celery, onion and broccoli in 2 ½ quart covered pan. Set aside. Blend cottage cheese in blender or processor until smooth. Slowly add milk while continuing to blend. Add chicken soup to cheese/milk mixture. Blend. Add broccoli mixture and heat through. Add salt and pepper. Yields 6 servings.

(Vern) Mary Ann Paul

CREAM OF ASPARAGUS SOUP

1 lb. asparagus
2 c. chicken broth
2 Tbsp. chopped onion
1 c. milk
ground pepper

Wash asparagus and cut into pieces. Cook in chicken broth and onion until tender. Puree in a blender. Return to pan and add milk and pepper.

If a thicker soup is desired, melt 2 tablespoons butter in a large pan. Add 2 tablespoons flour and cook until smooth. Slowly add milk. Add the asparagus puree and reheat until thickened.

Barbara King

TOMATO SOUP

6 onions
1 bunch celery
8 qt. fresh tomatoes
1 c. sugar
¼ c. salt
1 c. butter
1 c. flour

Cook tomatoes, onions and chopped celery until tender. Put through strainer. Add sugar and salt. Cream butter and flour and add to juice. Blend well and simmer until slightly thickened. Cook as long as you do for gravy. Put boiling soup in jars and seal. When serving, add a pinch of baking soda. Heat slightly, stirring in an equal amount of milk. Makes 12 pints.

Sylvia Stoltzfus
Mary Stoltzfus
Linda Fisher

TOMATO SOUP

5 qt. tomato juice
6 onions
1 stalk celery
2 peppers
½ c. sugar
⅓ c. salt

Boil the tomato juice, onions, celery and peppers until soft, then put through fruit press. Add the sugar and salt. Heat to boiling. Put in jars and seal.

Fannie Glick

HEARTY HAMBURGER SOUP

2 Tbsp. butter
1 c. chopped onions
1 c. sliced carrots
½ c. chopped green pepper
1 lb. ground beef
2 c. tomato juice
1 c. diced potatoes
1 ½ tsp. salt
1 tsp. seasoned salt
½ tsp. pepper
⅓ c. flour
4 c. milk

421792

Melt butter in a saucepan. Brown meat and add onion and cook until transparent. Stir in remaining ingredients except flour and milk. Cover and cook over low heat until vegetables are tender, about 20 to 25 minutes. Combine flour with 1 cup milk. Stir into soup mixture. Boil. Add remaining milk and heat, stirring frequently. Do not boil after adding remaining milk.

Mrs. Edna B. Zook

HAMBURGER SOUP

1 lb. ground beef
¼ c. chopped onions
18 oz. tomato juice
1 c. sliced raw carrots
1 beef bouillon cube
1 ½ tsp. salt
1 c. raw, diced potatoes
⅓ c. flour
4 c. milk
2 Tbsp. snipped parsley
green peppers, seasoned salt and butter may be added

Brown meat. Drain off fat. Add onions and cook until crisp-tender. Stir in tomato juice, carrots, bouillon cube and salt. Cover and simmer about 10 minutes. Add potatoes and parsley. Cook until vegetables are tender. Blend flour with 1 cup milk. Stir into soup. Cook and stir until thickened and bubbly. Add remaining milk and heat. Season to taste.

Barbara King
Edna Zook

HAM SOUP

4 c. ham, cubed
¾ c. onion
large handful noodles
2 medium size potatoes
3 qt. milk

Combine ham and onion. Cook until ham is soft and brown. Cut potatoes in small cubes. Add a little salt and cook until soft. Cook noodles in salt water until soft. Drain. Add to ham. Also add milk. Bring to a boil. Add salt and pepper. Serve with crackers.

Mrs. Edna B. Zook
Priscilla King

HAM AND BEAN SOUP

2 lb. beans
2 medium potatoes
1 lb. ham
salt to your taste

Soak beans overnight. Put water over beans and bring to a boil. Drain and add new water. Add potatoes and your cooked ham. Add your salt.

Priscilla King

EASY HAM AND BEAN SOUP

Use leftover ham. Add onions, celery and parsley, then add (canned) Great Northern beans (as many as desired) and cook until soft. Add milk and brown butter. Thicken with flour.

Sylvia Stoltzfus

BAKED BEAN SOUP

1 can baked beans
2 ½ c. milk
1 tsp. mustard
2 Tbsp. ketchup
1 Tbsp. butter
⅔ c. brown sugar
onions, as desired
bacon or ham cubes

Fry bacon or ham before putting into the soup.

Anna King

VEGETABLE SOUP

2 qt. potatoes
1 qt. lima beans
1 qt. corn
1 qt. carrots
½ qt. celery, cut fine
1 c. onions
½ qt. cauliflower
1 qt. peas
1 c. brown sugar
2 qt. tomato juice or V-8 juice
2 lb. ground meat
salt and pepper to taste

Mix together and put in jars. Cold pack 2 to 2 ½ hours. Alphabet noodles or small bow ties can be added, too, if desired. Cook them before adding.

Katie King
(Hammertown)

VEGETABLE SOUP

1 qt. string beans
1 qt. carrots
1 qt. potatoes
1 qt. celery, soak 1 hour
1 qt. onions
1 qt. corn
1 qt. peas
4 qt. tomato juice
2 qt. V-8 juice
2 Tbsp. bouillon
1 Tbsp. chili powder
½ c. brown sugar
3 lb. hamburg
beef cubes or beef broth (if preferred)

Fry the hamburg. Cook all vegetables separate. Mix all vegetables together. Cook juices and other ingredients with 1 package A-B-C noodles. Can for 2 ½ hours. Makes 12 quarts.

Barbie Zook
Rachel Esh
Linda Fisher

POTATO CHOWDER

4 c. diced potatoes
½ c. chopped onion
1 c. grated carrots
1 tsp. salt
¼ tsp. pepper
1 Tbsp. parsley
4 chicken bouillon cubes
4 Tbsp. butter
½ c. flour
6 c. scalded milk

In a large kettle combine potatoes, onion, carrots, salt, pepper, parsley flakes and bouillon cubes. Add enough water to cover vegetables. Cook until tender. Do not drain. Scald milk. Melt butter and add flour. Gradually stir in 1 ½ cups scalded milk. Add remaining hot to vegetables, then stir in thickened milk mixture. Stir until blended.

Mary Ann Smucker

POTATO RIVVEL SOUP

1 medium size onion
5 medium potatoes, diced
salt and pepper
2 eggs, beaten
1 tsp. salt

Cook potatoes and onions in water until potatoes are soft. To make rivvels, take 2 beaten eggs and salt. Add flour until the mixture is lumpy and dry. Sift excess flour out of rivvels, then dump rivvels into potato mixture and boil 5 minutes. Add:

½ stick butter
⅛ tsp. celery seed
1 to 1 ½ qt. milk
pinch of parsley

Heat and serve.

Mary Stoltzfus

POTATO SALAD

1 c. white sugar
¼ c. vinegar
¼ c. water
3 eggs

Boil together. Add as much salad dressing as juice (when cold).

Sylvia Petersheim

PINEAPPLE SALAD

1 large can pineapple, drained
2 oranges
2 or 3 c. miniature marshmallows
1 c. nuts
1 c. whipped cream
2 Tbsp. flour
2 eggs
½ c. sugar
pineapple juice

Cook the flour, eggs, sugar and pineapple juice together and chill.

Rachel Esh

TACO SALAD

1 lb. hamburg
tortilla chips
1 can kidney beans
1 c. sour cream
1 pkg. taco seasoning
lettuce
tomatoes
peppers
onions

Cheese Sauce:

¼ c. butter
½ lb. Velveeta cheese
¾ c. sour cream

Brown hamburg. Add taco seasoning. Mix and simmer according to package instruction. Layer bottom of platter with tortilla chips. Add hamburg and kidney beans. Spread 1 cup sour cream. Add lettuce, tomatoes, peppers and onions.

To Make Cheese Sauce: Melt butter and cheese together. Add sour cream and mix well. Pour over top of salad.

Mary Ann Smucker

QUICK AND EASY FRUIT SALAD

1 can pineapple chunks (15 oz. can)
1 can chunky mixed fruit (16 oz.)
1 pkg. instant vanilla pudding mix
3 Tbsp. instant orange flavored breakfast drink (Tang)
2 large bananas, sliced

121792

Drain pineapple and mixed fruit, reserving pineapple juice. Combine pudding mix, Tang and pineapple juice. Stir well. Combine with fruit and toss gently. Chill.

Mae Gay
Brooks, OR

GOLDEN EASTER EGGS

1 doz. hard-boiled eggs
3 Tbsp. yellow mustard
⅔ c. sugar
pinch of salt
2 c. vinegar
1 c. water

Mix together and boil 5 to 10 minutes. Add to eggs. Refrigerate overnight.

Susie S. King

BROCCOLI SALAD

1 large head broccoli, cut up
1 medium onion, chopped
8 slices bacon
½ c. cheese, cut up
1 c. mayonnaise
¼ to ½ c. sugar
2 to 3 Tbsp. vinegar

Cut bacon in bits and fry. Mix with mayonnaise, sugar and vinegar. Pour over rest of ingredients and let stand for 1 hour or more before serving. May add raisins, too.

Rachel Esh
Linda Fisher

CAULIFLOWER SALAD

1 head cauliflower
1 head broccoli
1 c. Velveeta cheese
10 to 12 slices bacon
1 c. mayonnaise
½ c. sugar
2 Tbsp. vinegar
2 tsp. mustard

Cut broccoli and cauliflower into small pieces. Fry bacon and crumble. Cut Velveeta cheese in small pieces. Mix the last 4 ingredients together and pour over top of cauliflower.

Elizabeth Stoltzfus

MACARONI SALAD

6 c. cooked elbow macaroni
¾ c. shredded carrots
½ c. diced celery
1 onion, diced
1 c. sugar
3 Tbsp. vinegar
1 tsp. salt
¼ tsp. pepper
2 tsp. mustard
mayonnaise

Mix all ingredients together and add enough mayonnaise to the right consistency. Chill overnight.

Linda Fisher

MACARONI AND POTATO SALAD

1 lb. cooked macaroni
1 c. sugar
¼ c. vinegar
2 Tbsp. mustard
2 c. mayonnaise
1 can condensed milk
1 grated onion
chopped carrots
chopped celery
6 hard-boiled eggs

Cream the macaroni, sugar, vinegar and mustard together. Combine in creamed mixture the remaining ingredients.

Naomi King

DELICIOUS POTATO SALAD

10 medium potatoes, cooked
5 eggs

Dressing:

1 ½ c. salad dressing
1 c. sugar
2 Tbsp. mustard
3 Tbsp. vinegar
1 ½ tsp. salt
1 tsp. celery seed
1 tsp. onion salt

Cool and dice potatoes and eggs. Pour mixed dressing over potatoes. Stir gently and let stand overnight.

Anna Fisher

APPLE SALAD

8 apples
½ c. raisins
1 c. marshmallows (miniature)
¼ c. coconut
½ c. nuts
juice of 1 lemon
1 c. water
1 tsp. vinegar
¼ tsp. salt
1 c. sugar
1 Tbsp. cornstarch
¼ c. cream
1 tsp. vanilla

121792

Dice apples. Place them in weak salt water while other ingredients are prepared or add lemon juice and mix thoroughly. Cook the water, vinegar, salt, sugar, cornstarch, cream and vanilla until slightly thickened.

Ruth Stoltzfus

APPLE SALAD

2 eggs, beaten
2 Tbsp. flour
1 c. water
1 c. sugar
2 tsp. butter
1 tsp. vanilla

Boil all together and cool. When ready to use, add apples, bananas, raisins and nuts.

Fannie Riehl
Susie King

APPLE SALAD

1 c. sugar
1 egg
1 Tbsp. flour
2 Tbsp. vinegar
1 c. water

Cook all ingredients together. Cool. Add small slices of apples and bananas.

Barbara King
Rachel Esh

LETTUCE SALAD

1 head lettuce
1 onion, minced
½ c. grated cheese
½ tsp. salt
2 ½ Tbsp. sugar
½ c. salad dressing
1 tsp. mustard
2 Tbsp. cream
1 tsp. vinegar

Chop lettuce. Put onion and cheese over top. Mix together salt, sugar, mustard and cream. Add vinegar and salad dressing. Pour over lettuce. (Eggs are a good substitute for the cheese.)

Mary Stoltzfus

MANDARIN SALAD

1 can drained mandarin oranges
1 small pkg. orange jello
1 small pkg. Philadelphia cream cheese
1 box Lucky Whip

Use juice to make orange jello. Let stand until partly set. Beat together cream cheese and Lucky Whip. Beat jello, cream cheese and Lucky Whip together until smooth. Stir in mandarin oranges.

Liz Stoltzfus

WATERGATE SALAD

3 ½ oz. pkg. pistachio pudding
9 oz. Cool Whip
20 oz. can crushed pineapple
½ c. small marshmallows

Put all ingredients in a bowl and mix together. Chill.

Liz Stoltzfus

CHRISTMAS SALAD

2 pkg. lime jello
1 can crushed pineapple, drain juice
3 c. water
2 pkg. Knox gelatine
⅔ c. cold water
1 cake Philadelphia cream cheese (8 oz.)
1 c. cream, sweetened to taste
2 pkg. cherry jello
3 ½ c. water

Mix together the lime jello, drained pineapple and water. Let set. Boil pineapple juice. Dissolve the gelatine in the cold water. Add to hot pineapple juice. Let cool. Combine the cream cheese and cream. Add to pineapple mixture. Let set. Mix the cherry jello and 3 ½ cups water.

Mrs. Elam Z. Stoltzfus
Priscilla Fisher

MOTHER'S DAY SALAD
(Very Good!!)

1 head lettuce
½ c. onions
½ c. peppers
8 strips bacon
2 c. cheese
4 hard-boiled eggs
½ c. frozen peas, raw

421792

Put your lettuce first, then your onions, peppers and cheese, then pour your dressing on. Top with hard-boiled eggs, bacon and peas. Let refrigerate overnight.

Dressing:

2 c. salad dressing
1 c. sugar
little vinegar
pinch of salt and pepper

Priscilla King

APRICOT SALAD

1 (1 lb.) can apricot halves
1 large can crushed pineapple
½ c. miniature marshmallows
1 box orange-pineapple jello
1 c. hot water
½ c. juice
¼ c. granulated sugar
1 ½ Tbsp. flour
½ c. mixed juice
1 egg
½ c. whipping cream

Dissolve jello in 1 cup hot water. Add ½ cup juice. Let cool, then add fruit and marshmallows. Put in an 8 x 8-inch pan. Let set several hours.

In a small pan, mix egg, ½ cup mixed juice, sugar and flour. Cook until thick. Cool. Whip the cream and add with cooked mixture. Pour over top of fruit.

Ruth Stoltzfus

OVERNIGHT FRUIT SALAD

1 lb. grapes, halved
1 lb. marshmallows, cut
1 small can crushed pineapple, drained
1 c. whipped cream
2 eggs
juice of 1 lemon
1 c. sugar

Mix fruits and marshmallows. Chill. Combine eggs, lemon and sugar. Cook over low heat until thickened. Cool. Fold in whipped cream. Fold cooked dressing into fruit mixture. Chill overnight.

Priscilla Fisher

PINEAPPLE SALAD

1 large can pineapple
2 oranges or apples (if desired)
small marshmallows
1 c. nuts
1 c. whipped cream
2 Tbsp. flour
2 eggs
½ c. sugar

Drain juice from pineapple and heat. When hot, add sugar, flour and beaten eggs to juice and cook until thick. Let cool, then whip the cream and add to mixture. Pour over fruit.

Sylvia Stoltzfus

CRANBERRY SUPREME SALAD

1 (13 oz.) pkg. raspberry Jell-O
1 c. boiling water
1 (16 oz.) can whole cranberry sauce
1 (13 oz.) pkg. lemon jello
1 c. boiling water
1 (3 oz.) pkg. cream cheese
⅓ c. mayonnaise
1 (8 ½ oz.) can crushed pineapple, undrained
1 c. whipping cream
1 c. miniature marshmallows

Dissolve raspberry Jell-O in 1 cup boiling water. Stir in cranberry sauce. Pour into bottom of a 1 ½ quart round mold. Chill until partially set. Dissolve lemon jello in 1 cup water. Set aside. Beat together cream cheese and mayonnaise. Gradually add lemon jello. Stir in pineapple and chill until partially set. Whip the whipping cream. Fold in lemon mixture. Add marshmallows. Spread lemon layer on top of cranberry mixture. Chill until set. Yields 12 servings.

Barbie Zook

COLE SLAW

2 c. cabbage, grated
¾ c. sugar
1 Tbsp. vinegar
½ tsp. salt
½ c. chopped celery
2 Tbsp. mayonnaise

Mix well.

Barbie Zook

DRESSING FOR TOSSED SALAD

3 Tbsp. sugar
1 tsp. salt
3 Tbsp. vinegar
2 Tbsp. salad oil

Combine ingredients. Stir to dissolve sugar. Pour dressing over vegetables and toss lightly.

Naomi Grace Zook

121792

LETTUCE DRESSING

2 c. white sugar
2/3 c. mayonnaise
1 can Carnation milk
1 Tbsp. vinegar
pinch of salt
mustard, may be added

Blend the sugar and mayonnaise well. Add the milk, vinegar and salt. May add mustard. This can be kept in refrigerator for up to 2 weeks.

Katie King
Fannie Riehl
Katie S. King
(Hammertown)

ANYTHING SALAD DRESSING

1/2 c. mayonnaise
1/4 c. sugar
1 Tbsp. vinegar

Sara Stoltzfus

BACON DRESSING

2 slices bacon, cut up
1 egg
3 Tbsp. sugar
3 Tbsp. vinegar

Fry bacon in a skillet. Beat egg, sugar and vinegar together. Cook and stir until thick in bacon drippings.

Elizabeth Stoltzfus

BARBECUE SAUCE

1 1/2 qt. vinegar
3/4 c. salt
1 1/2 pt. oil
1 qt. boiling water

Brush or spray on chicken every time you turn chicken. Sprinkle pepper over both sides of chicken when about halfway done. Mixture for 1 case of chicken.

Aarianne Petersheim

BARBECUED MEAT BALLS SAUCE

1 Tbsp. Worcestershire sauce
1/4 c. vinegar
3 Tbsp. sugar
1 1/2 c. ketchup
1/2 c. water
1/2 c. onion

Pour this mixture over meat balls and bake for 1 hour.

Rachel King

SPAGHETTI SAUCE

(My Own)

2 qt. tomato juice
1 pt. stewed tomatoes
2 c. chopped green pepper
1 chopped onion
chopped celery
1 large can tomato puree
1 large can Italian tomatoes
2 cans tomato paste
garlic and sugar to taste
salt and pepper
couple of bay leaves

Add the onion and celery if they are not included with the stewed tomatoes. Cook all ingredients until it boils and then low heat (simmer) for a couple of hours.

I cook my meatballs in with the sauce. Give better flavor. Fry the meatballs first, then put in the sauce.

(Vern) Mary Ann Paul

-• EXTRA RECIPES •-

421792

Hints for the Sink

Can't remove those yellow spots from sinks or dishes? Try this easy way: if salt does not work, sprinkle a small amount of cream of tartar and rub the particular area with a halved lemon, juice side down. Very good if you're in a hard water area.

If your sink is stainless steel and must be cleaned frequently, indeed, after each use, wash with hot water and a small quantity of detergent, using a sponge or cloth. But for small spots, apply sodium bicarbonate (baking soda) or a mild, nonabrasive soap powder. Never use steel wool or scouring pads on your stainless steel sink.

Residents of northern states should flush out their sink pipes at lease once a month during the cold winter months to prevent possible clogging due to ice formation and needless plumbing expense. Simply put a small amount of lye into the pipe and follow with 2 or 3 gallons of hot water.

To clear a sink or basin drain, trying using 1/2 cup of salt followed by boiling water. A slow-draining sink or basin calls for 2 or 3 tablespoonfuls of salt and 1/3 to 1/2 cup of vinegar. Allow to rest a few minutes and follow with hot water. In 1 hour, treat again with salt.

To disinfect a sink, clean with a hot solution of salt. Saves on scouring powder and bleach.

Keep the sink pipe dry and thus free of insects by ringing it with powdered charcoal.

Meat & Main Dishes

"Why are you so thankful, Hubby," my *better half*
asked me last night.
Then she laughed because I told her,
"Thankful for my appetite!"

Lord, yesterday I asked for all things
that I may enjoy life.
Today you gave me life
that I may enjoy all things.

Doctors all agree that the best and most wholesome part of a doughnut is the hole. The larger the hole the better the doughnut!

MEATS & MAIN DISHES

ADD A PINCH OF LOVE

Would you add just one thing more
To that recipe of yours
Before you give the oven door a shove?
It will make the whole thing lighter,
And your task will be the brighter
With a little, just a little pinch of love.

In your cooking and your baking
There is pleasure for the taking
If you first will ask a blessing from above
Keep ingredients to the letter
And your recipe is better
With a little, just a little pinch of love.

Rachel Esh

GROUND BEEF CHEESE BALLS

2 lb. ground beef
2 3/4 c. cracker crumbs
2 Tbsp. parsley flakes
1 tsp. salt
1/4 tsp. pepper
1 can condensed vegetable soup (10 oz.)
1 c. cold milk
cheese
pizza sauce

Mix all ingredients together except cheese and pizza sauce. Cut cheese into cubes. Put a cheese cube into the center of each meat ball and put in baking pan. Add a little water. Bake at 400° for 30 minutes. Add pizza sauce and grated cheese. Bake 15 minutes longer.

Fannie Riehl

PORCUPINE MEAT BALLS

1 lb. ground beef
1/2 c. rice
1 Tbsp. salt
1 Tbsp. pepper
1 chopped onion
2 cans tomato soup
1/2 c. water
1 tsp. sugar

Wash rice. Combine meat, rice, salt, pepper and onion and shape into small meat balls. Heat tomato soup with water and sugar in cooker. Drop meat balls into soup mixture and place cover on cooker and cook until done or if you have a pressure cooker, 10 minutes.

(Vern) Mary Ann Paul

MEAT LOAF OR MEAT BALLS

hamburg (as much as you need)

Ingredients For 1 lb. Hamburg:

1 egg
1 onion, chopped (small)
celery, chopped (1 large stalk)
salt and pepper
bread crumbs
ketchup
garlic and grated cheese to taste (if desired)

Use enough bread crumbs and ketchup to work it. Mix all together. Bake meat loaf at 350° for 1 hour.

For Meat balls: Fry slow, then no oil is needed. It will fry in its own juices.

(Vern) Mary Ann Paul

MEAT LOAF

1 ½ lb. hamburger
1 c. soft bread crumbs or oatmeal
1 c. milk or tomato juice
1 medium size onion, minced
1 or 2 eggs, beaten
1 tsp. salt
⅛ tsp. pepper
6 strips bacon (may be added)

Soak crumbs in milk and add beaten egg(s). Add meat, onion and seasoning. Form into a loaf (do not pack) and place in baking dish, then put strips of bacon on top of loaf. Bake at 375° for 1 hour. Serves 6.

Sylvia Stoltzfus
Edna Zook

MEAT LOAF

1 ½ lb. ground beef
1 c. fresh bread crumbs
1 chopped onion
1 egg
1 tsp. salt
½ tsp. pepper
2 tsp. prepared mustard
2 tsp. Worcestershire sauce
3 Tbsp. vinegar
3 Tbsp. brown sugar
2 cans Hunt's tomato sauce or tomato juice

Mix together beef, crumbs, onion, beaten egg, salt, pepper and ½ can sauce. Form into loaf and put in shallow pan. Combine rest of ingredients and pour over meat. Bake at 350° for 1 hour and 15 minutes.

Priscilla Fisher

MEAT LOAF

2 lb. hamburger
1 ½ c. cornflake crumbs
2 tsp. salt
½ tsp. pepper
¼ c. brown sugar
½ c. ketchup
2 eggs
milk until moist

Bake at 350° for 1 hour and 15 minutes.

Fannie Riehl

MOCK HAM LOAF

1 lb. hamburger
½ lb. hot dogs, ground fine
1 c. cracker crumbs
1 tsp. salt
dash of pepper
1 egg

Combine all ingredients. Add ½ of the glaze mixture to ingredients. Mix well. Shape into a loaf. Bake at 350° for 1 ½ hours. Baste occasionally with the glaze.

Glaze:

¾ c. brown sugar
½ c. water
½ tsp. mustard
1 Tbsp. vinegar

Naomi Petersheim
Naomi Grace Zook
Rachel King
Susie King
Linda Fisher

CHICKEN CROQUETTES

White Sauce:

2 Tbsp. butter
2 ½ Tbsp. flour
1 c. milk

Make the sauce and cool.

2 c. ground chicken
1 tsp. salt
¼ tsp. onion juice
⅛ tsp. pepper
onion salt or celery salt may be added

Add the white sauce to the remaining ingredients. Shape into patties or balls and dip into beaten eggs and roll in cracker crumbs. Deep fry.

Mrs. Edna B. Zook
Nancy Ann Esch
Anna Fisher

FISH CROQUETTES

3 Tbsp. butter
1 Tbsp. flour
¾ c. milk
2 eggs
1 ½ c. flaked fish (cooked or canned)
½ tsp. salt

Roll croquettes in 2 cups dry bread crumbs. Deep fry.

Susie S. King

BARBECUE

1 lb. hamburger
1 onion
salt and pepper
1 Tbsp. pepper
1 Tbsp. sugar
½ c. catsup or chili sauce
1 spoon mustard
1 tsp. celery seed

Saute hamburger, onion, salt and pepper until brown, then add the remaining ingredients and simmer for 1 hour.

(Vern) Mary Ann Paul

HAMBURGERS

1 lb. ground beef
½ c. cracker crumbs
2 eggs
1 c. milk
salt and pepper
onions (if desired)

Drop by tablespoon into a greased frying pan. Turn when bottom side is firm and brown. Continue frying until done.

Liz Stoltzfus

BARBECUED HAMBURGER

2 lb. hamburger
1 onion
½ c. catsup
2 Tbsp. brown sugar
2 Tbsp. vinegar
2 tsp. mustard
1 tsp. Worcestershire sauce
1 tsp. salt

Fry onion and hamburger until it has lost its raw, red color. Add rest of ingredients. Simmer about 20 minutes and serve with hamburger rolls. Can be made ahead of time, then just reheated.

Nancy Ann Esch

OVEN CRUSTED CHICKEN

- ½ c. butter or margarine, melted (1 stick)
- ⅓ c. all-purpose flour
- 1 ½ tsp. salt
- ⅛ tsp. thyme
- ⅛ tsp. rosemary, crushed
- ⅛ tsp. marjoram
- 5 c. Kountry Fresh corn flakes cereal, crushed to 1 ½ c.
- 2 ½ to 3 lb. cut up broiler-fryer chicken, skinned

Preheat oven to 375°. In a medium bowl combine butter, flour, salt, thyme, rosemary and marjoram. In shallow dish place cereal. Dip chicken in butter mixture. Roll in cereal to coat. Place on rack in shallow baking pan. Bake 55 to 60 minutes or until golden brown. Makes 6 servings.

Sara Stoltzfoos

LEMONY CHICKEN BREASTS

- 1 boneless, skinless whole chicken breast, cut in half lengthwise (approximately 10 oz.)
- 1 Tbsp. all-purpose flour
- ¼ tsp. each salt and pepper
- 2 tsp. olive oil
- ⅓ c. chicken broth
- 2 Tbsp. lemon juice
- 1 Tbsp. chopped parsley

Coat chicken with a mixture of the flour, salt and pepper. Heat oil in a large skillet over medium-high heat. Add chicken and cook 6 to 8 minutes, turning once, until lightly browned and no longer pink in center when tested with tip of a knife. Remove to serving platter or dinner plates. Add chicken broth and lemon juice to skillet. Stir over medium-high heat 2 to 3 minutes, scraping up any browned bits in pan, until sauce is reduced slightly. Stir in parsley. Pour over chicken. Makes 2 servings.

Rebecca K. Stoltzfus

CHICKEN LOAF

- 1 qt. canned chicken
- 1 c. cooked rice
- 2 c. bread crumbs
- 4 eggs, beaten
- 2 c. chicken broth
- 1 c. cream of mushroom soup
- 1 c. cream of celery soup

Combine ingredients and bake, uncovered, at 350° for 1 hour.

Susie S. King

CHEESEBURGER LOAVES

2 c. cornflakes cereal
1 egg
1 (8 oz.) can stewed tomatoes
1 tsp. salt
⅛ tsp. pepper
1 lb. ground beef
3 slices cheese, cut in half

Measure cornflakes cereal. Crush to 1 cup. Place in a large mixing bowl. Add egg, tomatoes, salt and pepper. Beat well. Add ground beef. Mix only until combined. Shape into 6 loaves, about 4-inches long. Place in a single layer in shallow pan. Bake in oven at 350° about 30 minutes. Remove from oven. Top loaves with ½ slice cheese. Return to oven. Bake 10 minutes or until cheese melts.

(Vern) Mary Ann Paul

BAKED HAM

3 or 4 slices ham (¾-inch thick)
2 Tbsp. dry mustard
4 Tbsp. brown sugar
milk to cover

Place ham slices in roast pan. Rub dry mustard and brown sugar on. Add enough milk to barely cover. Bake at 350° for 1 to 1 ½ hours. This is delicious!

Elsie Kauffman

BARBECUE SAUCE FOR CHICKEN

1 pt. water
1 c. vinegar
¼ c. salt
1 Tbsp. brown sugar
½ tsp. red pepper
1 tsp. black pepper
¼ oz. Worcestershire sauce
½ lb. butter
½ tsp. paprika

Melt and cool butter. Add other ingredients. Brush or sprinkle on chicken. Broil over hot coals or grill, turning frequently, until done, about 1 to 1 ½ hours. Put sauce on every time you turn it. This is enough for 20 legs and thighs combined. Leftover sauce can be stored in the refrigerator.

Ruth Stoltzfus

BARBECUE CHICKEN

(50 Pieces)

¾ lb. butter
4 tsp. salt
3 c. vinegar

Sauce to brush on 20 minutes before done. Ten minutes each side.

½ c. lemon juice
1 Tbsp. salt
1 tsp. pepper
¼ c. brown sugar
¾ c. mustard
1 c. ketchup
1 ½ sticks butter

Fannie Riehl

PORK CHOPS (BREADED)

6 pork chops
¾ c. fine bread crumbs
1 tsp. salt
⅛ tsp. pepper
1 egg, beaten
¼ c. milk
¼ c. boiling water

Add salt and pepper to bread crumbs. Beat egg and add milk. Dip chops in liquid and roll in crumbs. Put 3 tablespoons lard in skillet and brown chops. Place chops in a small roasting pan and add boiling water. Cover and bake at 400° for 50 to 60 minutes.

Katie King
(Hammertown)

BAKED LIVER

1 lb. thinly sliced liver
salt and pepper to season

Dip liver in flour. Brown in frying pan, then place in casserole dish.

Sauce:

1 large onion, chopped
1 Tbsp. butter
2 tsp. dry mustard
4 tsp. sugar
½ c. ketchup
2 Tbsp. vinegar
½ c. water

Cook sauce 10 minutes. Pour over liver and bake at 350° for 1 hour.

Susie S. King

421792

POOR MAN'S STEAK

1 to 2 lb. hamburg
1 c. milk
¼ tsp. pepper
1 c. cracker crumbs
1 tsp. salt
1 small onion, chopped

Mix well and shape into narrow loaf. Let set for 8 hours or overnight. Slice and fry in a little butter or oil until brown. Put slices in layers in roaster and spread cream of mushroom soup on each piece. (Use 1 can in all.) Bake 1 hour at 325°.

Katie King
(Willie) Anna Fisher
(Hammertown)

CHILI

1 lb. hamburg
½ c. brown sugar
2 Tbsp. mustard
1 medium onion
2 cans kidney beans
1 pt. tomato juice
salt and pepper
1 scant Tbsp. chili powder

Brown the hamburg, brown sugar, mustard and onion. Add the remaining ingredients and simmer 1 hour.

Aarianne Petersheim

CREAMED DRIED BEEF

4 Tbsp. butter
¼ lb. dried beef
4 Tbsp. flour
2 ½ c. milk

Melt butter in skillet and put beef in to brown. Dust beef with flour. Let that mixture brown. Add milk gradually, stirring constantly, while cooking over a low heat. Cook until gravy has thickened and is smooth. This is good with toast and eggs.

Mary Stoltzfus

TURKEY OR CHICKEN STUFFING

2 lb. bread cubes
1 doz. eggs, beat well
1 lb. butter
1 stalk celery, chopped into small pieces
salt and pepper to taste

Melt butter, then add celery and cook until soft. Mix eggs, salt and pepper with bread cubes, then add celery. Mix well.

Nancy Ann Esch

36 ROASTS

36 gal. filling
1 ½ gal. celery
3 scant Tbsp. pepper
16 scant Tbsp. salt
7 lb. butter
½ gal. Fluffo (I like lard)
about 5 doz. eggs

We put the butter in the iron kettle and let it get brown, then put your lard in, salt, pepper, celery, liver, hearts and stomach. (I cook that in kettle first, then grind it.) Put in iron kettle and let it all cook for a little while. Pour over bread, also, your egg mixture. Stir just to mix it. If you stir too much, it will get soggy. (I put some milk with the egg mixture.)

Katie King

BARBECUE DOGGIES

¼ c. chopped onion
1 Tbsp. vinegar
½ tsp. flour
1 Tbsp. Worcestershire sauce
1 Tbsp. brown sugar
2 Tbsp. water
½ tsp. chili powder
¼ c. ketchup
hot dogs

Mix all ingredients together except hot dogs. Slit the hot dogs and bake in sauce 20 to 25 minutes at 350°. Turn hot dogs once while baking. Serve in sauce.

Mary Stoltzfus

IMPOSSIBLE CHEESEBURGER PIE

1 lb. ground beef or 1 pt. canned beef
chopped onion to suit your taste
½ tsp. salt
¼ tsp. pepper
1 c. shredded cheese (any white kind)
1 ½ c. milk
¾ c. Bisquick
3 eggs

Heat oven to 400°. Grease a 10-inch pie plate. Cook and stir beef and onion until brown. Put in plate. Sprinkle with cheese. Beat remaining ingredients until smooth. Pour over beef and cheese. Bake 30 minutes.

Linda Fisher

121792

QUICK CHICKEN PIE

1 fat hen

Sauce:

3 Tbsp. butter
3 Tbsp. flour
2 c. chicken broth
1 c. milk

Cook hen tender. Cut from bones. Put in baking pan. Add 1 bag of mixed vegetables. Cook sauce until thick as gravy, season and pour over chicken and vegetables.

Batter:

2 c. flour
2 Tbsp. shortening
2 tsp. baking powder
1 tsp. salt
1 egg
1 c. milk

Mix flour, shortening, baking powder and salt, then add egg and milk. (Mix well.) Spread over chicken. Bake at 350° for 40 minutes or until done.

Susie King

CHICKEN CHEESE PIE

2 c. diced, cooked chicken
1 (9-inch) unbaked pie shell
1 c. shredded Swiss cheese
4 eggs, slightly beaten
1 c. milk
¼ c. melted butter
½ tsp. onion salt
½ tsp. salt
⅛ tsp. ground nutmeg
2 Tbsp. grated Romano cheese
2 strips bacon, cooked, drained and crumbled
1 Tbsp. minced fresh parsley

Layer chicken in pie shell. Sprinkle with cheese. Combine eggs, milk, butter, onion salt, salt and nutmeg. Beat with rotary eggbeater or whisk until blended. Pour over chicken and cheese. Sprinkle with Romano cheese. Bake in a 425° oven for 10 minutes. Reduce heat to 325° for 30 minutes or until crust is golden brown and a knife inserted in center comes out clean. Sprinkle with bacon and parsley. Makes 6 to 8 servings.

Rebecca K. Stoltzfus

CHICKEN PIE

Filling:

3 Tbsp. butter
3 Tbsp. flour
1 tsp. salt
⅛ tsp. pepper
2 c. milk
2 c. chopped chicken, cooked
1 ½ pt. frozen vegetables

Biscuit Topping:

2 c. sifted flour
3 tsp. baking powder
1 tsp. salt
1 tsp. paprika
⅓ c. shortening
⅔ c. milk

Melt butter in saucepan. Stir in flour, salt and pepper. Remove from heat and gradually stir in milk. Return to heat and cook until smooth and slightly thick (stirring constantly). Add chicken and vegetables. Pour in baking dish. Mix top and roll out. Cover the chicken and vegetables. Cut in slits to allow steam to escape. Bake at 425° for 20 minutes or until golden brown.

Mary Stoltzfus

IMPOSSIBLE HAM IN SWISS PIE

2 c. cut up fully cooked ham
1 c. shredded natural Swiss cheese
⅓ c. chopped onions
4 eggs
2 c. milk
1 c. Bisquick
salt
pepper

Heat oven to 400°. Grease a 9-inch pie plate. Sprinkle ham, cheese and onions in plate. Beat remaining ingredients until smooth. Pour into plate. Bake 35 to 40 minutes.

Sylvia Petersheim

IMPOSSIBLE CHEESEBURGER PIE

1 lb. ground beef or 1 qt. canned beef
chopped onion to taste
½ tsp. salt
¼ tsp. pepper
1 c. shredded cheese (any kind)
1 ½ c. milk
¾ c. Bisquick
3 eggs

Heat oven to 400°. Grease a 10-inch pie plate. Cook and stir beef and onion until brown. Put in plate. Sprinkle with cheese. Beat

421792

remaining ingredients until smooth, then pour in pie plate. Bake 30 minutes. No longer!

Naomi Grace Zook

POTATO PIZZA BAKE

1 lb. ground beef
4 c. thinly sliced potatoes
1 medium onion, chopped
1 can Cheddar cheese soup
1 soup can milk
1 can tomato sauce (15 oz.)
salt and pepper to taste
½ tsp. oregano
½ tsp. sugar
6 oz. Mozzarella cheese
½ c. Parmesan cheese

Brown beef in pan. Place potatoes and onion in baking dish. Add meat. Mix soup, milk, tomato sauce, salt, pepper, oregano and sugar. Pour on top. Do not stir. Dot with butter. Bake, covered, at 375° for 1 hour. Remove from oven and arrange cheese on top. Return to oven, uncovered, for about 15 minutes until cheese is melted.

Linda Fisher

SAVORY BEEF CASSEROLE

2 lb. round beef cubes
¼ c. cooking oil
1 ½ c. chopped onion
1 (1 lb.) can tomatoes
3 Tbsp. quick cooking tapioca
1 (10 ½ oz.) can condensed beef broth
1 clove garlic, minced
1 Tbsp. parsley flakes
2 ½ tsp. salt
¼ tsp. pepper
1 bay leaf
6 medium carrots, cut into strips
3 medium potatoes, pared and cut in quarters
½ c. sliced celery

Brown beef cubes on all sides in hot oil in large skillet. Add onion, tomatoes, tapioca, beef broth, garlic, parsley, salt, pepper and bay leaf. Bring mixture to a boil. Turn into a 3 quart casserole. Cover. Bake at 350° for 1 hour and 30 minutes or until meat is tender. Add carrots, potatoes and celery. Continue baking, covered, for 1 hour or until vegetables are tender.

Linda Fisher

LEFTOVER DISH

3 c. bread crumbs
⅓ c. melted butter
1 egg, beaten with a little milk

In a baking dish, mix any leftovers you have, meats, vegetables or whatever. Meat with gravy makes a tasty dish. Mix the bread crumbs, butter and egg. Season with salt and pepper. Some crumbled dried celery leaves are also good. Put this mixture on top. Cheese added to the vegetables or on top of the bread crumbs is also good. Bake 1 hour at 350°.

Elsie Kauffman

SPANISH RICE

1 lb. hamburg
1 small chopped onion
½ c. diced green pepper
1 c. rice, cooked
½ c. diced cheese
½ tsp. chili powder
salt and pepper to taste
dash of oregano

Mix all together and put into casserole. Add tomato juice (diluted with water) to cover. Bake for 1 hour at 350°.

Peppers may be stuffed with the hamburg, rice, cheese, salt, pepper, oregano and chili powder. Set in diluted tomato juice to bake.

Linda Fisher

STUFFED CABBAGE

1 large head cabbage
2 lb. hamburger
½ c. rice, cooked
2 eggs
2 cans tomato soup

Core cabbage and bring the water to a boil with the whole head of cabbage. Pour off water. Cool cabbage. Mix hamburger, rice and eggs. Carefully remove cabbage leaves and roll hamburger mixture in each leaf. Put in large pot. Add diluted tomato soup. Cook for 2 hours on small light. Makes about 20 rolls.

Louise Utter

TUNA-BROCCOLI SUPREME

2 (10 oz.) pkg. chopped broccoli
2 cans cream of mushroom soup
⅔ c. milk
⅓ c. lemon juice
2 (7 oz.) cans tuna, drained
1 c. crushed potato chips

Cook broccoli in boiling salted water until all pieces are separated. Drain. Blend together soup and milk. Stir in lemon juice and

421792

tuna. Add broccoli. Spoon into greased 2 ½ quart casserole. Top with crushed potato chips. Bake in moderate oven (350°) until bubbling, about 30 minutes.

Rebecca Stoltzfus

TUNA NOODLE CASSEROLE

Velveeta cheese
½ c. milk
2 c. cooked noodles, drained
1 (6 ½ oz.) can tuna
½ c. bread crumbs
4 Tbsp. butter, melted

Mix noodles and tuna together. Pour milk over it. Put a layer of Velveeta cheese over top. Top with bread crumbs tossed in butter. The thin kind of noodles are preferred. Bake at 325° for 30 to 40 minutes.

Elizabeth Stoltzfus

TUNA AND MACARONI

1 lb. elbow macaroni
tuna
1 can mushroom soup
milk
bread crumbs

Cook macaroni according to directions. Pat part of macaroni into greased casserole dish. Add tuna chunks over this. Pour ⅓ can mushroom soup. Repeat until dish is full. Pour milk over all until it covers the macaroni. Top with bread crumbs. Bake 1 hour in moderate oven. Cheese slices may be put on top for last 10 minutes of baking instead of bread crumbs.

Sylvia Stoltzfus

CHICKEN CASSEROLE

32 slices bread
9 lb. chicken, cooked and deboned
2 c. onion
1 Tbsp. salt
2 c. mayonnaise
2 c. celery
½ tsp. pepper

Cut bread into 1-inch cubes. Put half into buttered baking dish and add chicken, then remaining cubes. Mix last 5 ingredients with 6 beaten eggs and 6 cups milk. Pour over bread and chicken. Let set at least 1 hour or overnight. Before baking, pour 4 cans of cream of mushroom soup over top. (Gravy made with chicken broth may be used instead of soup.) If desired, top with grated cheese for the last ½ hour of baking. Bake at 325° for 1 hour. Enough for 24 people.

Elizabeth Stoltzfus

HAMBURGER POT PIE

Onion Pastry:

2 c. flour
¾ c. Crisco
1 tsp. onion salt
¼ c. cold water

Bake at 400° for 25 minutes or until crust is brown.

Pie Filling:

1 Tbsp. Crisco
1 lb. ground beef
½ c. chopped onion
1 (15 or 16 oz.) can green beans, drained or 2 c. fresh or frozen beans
1 tsp. salt
1 Tbsp. sugar
¼ tsp. pepper
⅛ tsp. oregano
1 (10 oz.) can tomato soup

In a skillet heat Crisco. Add beef and onion. Cook just until meat is brown. Stir in green beans, soup and seasonings. Pour filling into onion pastry. Place top crust over the filling.

(Vern) Mary Ann Paul

HAMBURG CASSEROLE

1 lb. hamburg
1 tsp. salt
1 onion
1 c. celery
1 can kidney beans
3 medium size potatoes
tomato soup
butter

Brown hamburg, onion, celery and salt until all redness is gone. Remove from heat and add kidney beans. Butter a nice size casserole. Cut potatoes like you would French fries. Put a layer of hamburg mixture, then potatoes, then hamburg again and onion. Pour tomato soup over all and dot with butter. Cover and bake in a 350° oven for 1 ½ hours.

Elsie Kauffman

421792

HAMBURG FILLING CASSEROLE

¼ lb. butter
3 pieces celery
1 small onion
1 ½ qt. bread, diced
2 eggs
½ c. milk
1 lb. hamburg
1 can cream of mushroom soup

Melt butter and add diced celery and onion. Dice bread and add beaten eggs and milk. Brown hamburg. Add salt and pepper. Put 3 layers filling and 2 layers hamburg. Pour mushroom soup on top. Bake 1 hour at 350°. Other soup or cheese sauce is also good on top.

Elizabeth Stoltzfus

HAM DINNER

1 ½ c. cubed ham
1 c. diced potatoes
1 c. diced peas or carrots
2 c. cooked noodles

Topping:

1 ½ c. flour
½ tsp. salt
3 tsp. baking powder
½ tsp. salt
2 Tbsp. shortening
¾ c. milk

Brown ham. Add other ingredients. Add enough boiling water to cover. Thicken with flour. Put mixture in casserole. Add topping. Bake at 350° for 20 to 30 minutes.

Topping: Mix and drop on top by tablespoon.

Fannie Riehl

ESCALLOPED POTATOES AND HAM

4 c. grated potatoes
1 c. ham, cubed
2 ½ c. milk
1 tsp. salt
pepper to taste
1 tsp. flour

Mix all ingredients in a casserole. Bake 1 to 1 ½ hours.

Barbie Zook

WIGGLERS

9 hot dogs or 9 slices bacon
3 c. diced potatoes
3 c. peas
3 c. celery
3 c. macaroni
3 c. carrots
2 cans cream of celery soup
1 lb. Velveeta cheese
3 lb. hamburger
3 onions

Fry onions and hamburger until brown. Cook all other vegetables separate. Mix together. Put in casserole. Top with cheese and hot dogs. Bake 1 ½ hours at 350°.

Mrs. Edna B. Zook
Mary Stoltzfus

SPAGHETTI AND MEAT BALLS

- 2 small cans tomato paste
- 2 small cans tomato sauce
- 1 qt. tomatoes
- 1 onion
- salt and pepper
- 1 to 2 lb. hamburger
- 2 eggs
- 2 lb. spaghetti

Combine first 3 ingredients, mixing 1 can of water to each can of paste. Cook slowly for 2 hours. Mix ½ cup bread crumbs with hamburger. Add eggs. Saute onion and add to hamburger. Make meat balls and fry in skillet. Add to spaghetti sauce. Cook spaghetti and add sauce. Will feed about 10 to 12 people.

Louise Utter

PIZZA CASSEROLE

- 1 lb. ground beef, fried
- 1 onion
- 1 scant tsp. oregano
- ½ tsp. salt
- 2 c. cooked noodles
- 1 can tomato soup
- ⅓ c. water
- 2 c. grated Velveeta cheese

Mix all ingredients together and bake at 350° for 30 to 40 minutes.

Linda Fisher

STROMBOLI

Dough:

- 1 Tbsp. yeast
- 1 c. warm water
- 1 tsp. salt
- ½ c. salad oil
- 3 c. flour (2 c. bread flour and 1 c. all-purpose flour)

Mix yeast and water, then let stand 5 minutes before adding rest of ingredients. Roll out into 4 strips about 8-inches wide by 12-inches long.

421792

Filling:

chipped ham
salami
Muenster or Mozzarella cheese
sweet peppers
mushrooms

Layer into center of each strip, grated cheese, ham, salami, cheese and peppers in order given, then mushrooms, then sprinkle with onion salt. Bring sides of dough up to the center and pinch together tightly (or it will separate while baking). Bake on cookie sheets at 350° for 20 to 30 minutes.

Nancy Ann Esch

LASAGNA

Sauce:

3 Tbsp. oil
1 c. chopped onion
1 lb. beef
pizza sauce
oregano, salt and pepper to taste

Cook lasagna noodles and cool off. Layer lasagna noodles, sauce and cheese. Make 3 layers of each. Nine noodles makes 1 pan. Bake at 350°.

Aarianne

STUFFED JUMBO SHELLS

20 to 24 jumbo macaroni shells (8 oz.)
1 egg, beaten
¾ c. soft bread crumbs
¼ c. parsley, snipped
1 Tbsp. onion, chopped
½ tsp. salt
1 lb. ground beef, fried soft
3 c. spaghetti sauce or tomato juice

Cook shells in boiling water and drain. In mixing bowl combine egg, crumbs, parsley, onion and salt. Add meat. Mix well. Stuff shells. Pour 1 ½ cups sauce or juice in bottom of a 13 x 9 x 2-inch pan. Arrange stuffed shells on sause and pour remaining sauce on top. Bake (uncovered) for 1 to 1 ¼ hours at 375°.

Linda Fisher

YUMZETTA

1 pkg. noodles, cooked (medium size)
3 lb. hamburger, brown in butter
1 pt. peas

Topping:

2 cans mushroom soup
1 can celery soup
1 c. sour cream
buttered bread crumbs

Butter pan and put in a layer of noodles, a layer of hamburger and a layer of peas. Mix soups and sour cream and pour over top. Top with buttered crumbs. Bake 1 hour at 300°.

Barbara King

CHICKENETTI

1 (8 oz.) box spaghetti
4 c. chicken
¼ c. chopped green peppers
2 cans cream of mushroom soup
1 c. chicken broth
1 small onion, chopped
½ tsp. salt
¼ tsp. pepper
2 c. shredded cheese

Cook spaghetti and add rest of ingredients. Pour into casserole dish. Bake at 350° for 1 hour.

Mary Ann Smucker

HAMBURG CASSEROLE

1 lb. hamburg, browned and drained
5 medium potatoes, diced and uncooked
1 onion, chopped
1 can vegetable soup
1 can tomato soup
1 can Cheddar cheese soup

Put hamburg in bottom of casserole, then potatoes and onion. Mix soups in separate bowl (do not add water). Pour over meat and potatoes. Bake at 325° for 1 hour.

Anna Fisher

OMELETS

4 eggs
4 Tbsp. milk
2 Tbsp. butter
½ tsp. salt
⅛ tsp. pepper

121792

Beat egg yolks. Add liquid and seasonings. Fold in egg whites. Cook over low heat until golden brown. Flip. Add cheese and meats, etc. Cut in half and fold over.

Naomi Petersheim

EGG OMELET

9 eggs
6 heaping Tbsp. flour
1 pt. water
½ tsp. salt

Beat eggs. Add flour and beat again. Add water and salt. Brown 1 stick butter in 2 (9-inch) cake pans. Pour egg mixture over butter. Bake at 400° for ¾ hour or until crusty and brown around the edge. May put bacon bits on top. Very good!

Susie S. King

BREAKFAST SPECIAL

½ lb. Swiss cheese
½ lb. white American cheese
1 can cream of mushroom soup
¾ lb. chipped ham
2 eggs per person
½ soup can milk

Beat eggs and grate the cheese. Mix everything together. Bake at 350° for 1 to 1 ¼ hours. Serves at least 8.

Other cheese may also be used for substitutes.

Elizabeth Stoltzfus

BREAKFAST SAUSAGE EGG DELIGHT

1 lb. sausage, browned and drained
5 eggs
6 slices bread, cubed
2 c. milk
1 Tbsp. dry mustard
1 tsp. salt
1 c. grated cheese

Mix this together. Let set overnight. Bake at 325° for 1 hour.

Anna Fisher

COUNTRY BRUNCH

16 slices firm white bread
2 ½ c. cooked, cubed ham (about 1 lb.)
16 oz. Mozzarella cheese
16 oz. Cheddar cheese
6 eggs
3 c. whole milk
½ tsp. dry mustard
⅛ to ¼ tsp. onion powder

Topping:

3 c. uncrushed corn flakes
½ c. melted butter

Trim crusts from bread. Break into pieces. Grease a 13 x 9 x 2-inch baking pan and layer as follows: 1 layer bread, 1 layer ham, 1 layer cheese and continue until all is used. Combine eggs, milk and seasoning. Pour over layers and refrigerate overnight. Remove from refrigerator 30 minutes before baking. Combine topping ingredients. Sprinkle over casserole. Cover loosely with foil. Bake at 375° for 45 minutes.

Priscilla King
Naomi King

STROMBOLI

Dough:

1 Tbsp. yeast
1 c. warm water
1 tsp. sugar
1 tsp. salt
2 Tbsp. oil
about 2 ½ c. bread flour

Dissolve yeast in warm water. Stir in remaining ingredients. Stir well. Let dough rest 5 minutes. Roll out dough in 2 parts. Sprinkle inside and outside with seasoned salt. Fill with ham and cheese or to taste. Peppers, onions or mushrooms may be added. Fold dough up over filling and put on cookie sheet. Bake 20 minutes at 400°.

Aarianne Petersheim
Ruth Stoltzfus

SCRABBLE

6 qt. rich, fresh pork broth
6 c. pudding meat
6 c. yellow cornmeal
3 c. white flour

Bring the pork broth and the pudding meat to a boil. Stir the cornmeal and flour into broth. Salt and pepper to taste. Continue to cook over medium heat for 2 hours.

Priscilla King

Potatoes

If you've made the mistake of boiling potatoes, do save the remaining water. Use it in place of milk in a cake recipe: the cake will keep fresh much longer. The liquor may also be used in soups, stews, casseroles, or marinating mixtures, or as a steaming liquid for other vegetables.

To make your baked potatoes a beautiful brown, wash the skins well, dry, and cover with vegetable oil before putting them into the oven. Place them on foil before heating.

Hope you'll no longer eat mashed boiled potatoes, which have lost nutrients in peeling and long cooking. Bake or steam them only. Potatoes steamed in their jackets can be mashed.

Do use the flat surface of a masher to stir sauces. Prevents scorching and keeps the bottom of the pan clean.

Peeled too many potatoes by mistake? Cover with cold water, add a little (brown or cider) vinegar, and refrigerate. They'll keep a few days.

Ever eat a potato sliced *raw* in a salad or soup?

To keep heather fresh, stick the stems in a raw potato.

If you think a potato is just for eating, I've got news for you: A thin slice of salted raw potato rubbed on hives or mosquito bites quickly relieves the itching.

For a fresh burn or scald, cut and apply a thin slice of this tuber to ease the pain and take the sting out of the burn.

To remove old and stubborn blackheads: mash a boiled potato into a pulp and, while hot, place some on cheesecloth and apply to the area to be treated. Repeat two or three times to adequately soften the blackheads and they'll be removed with ease.

Remove vegetable stains from your hands by rubbing with a cut raw potato.

Rubbed on a painted surface, potato will remove pencil grease and other tricky spots.Wipe with damp cloth or sponge.

Vegetables

Said a squash to a turnip, one bright summerday,,
"Let us hide for I see the cook coming this way."
The Way to a Man's Heart Cookbook is under her arm.
The look in her eyes fills my heart with alarm."
"Foolish squash," said the turnip "why raise all the fuss?
Of course she is coming and coming for us,
Ere she cuts off my tops and my roots, I will pause,
To say if we die it is for a good cause!"

Life is like a piano - what you get out of it depends on how you play it.

Ants

An ant problem may be solved by sprinkling about a mixture of powdered cloves and red pepper, with or without sulfur. Or prepare an old-fashioned but still effective insect or ant powder: mix thoroughly, equal parts of borax, pyrethum, and pepper. Dry the affected area and the threshold and spread lightly.

VEGETABLES

THE VEGETABLE GARDENS

First Plant Five Rows of Peas:

Patience
Promptness
Preparation
Perseverance
Purity

Next Plant Three Rows of Squash:

Squash gossip
Squash criticism
Squash indifference

Then Plant Five Rows of Lettuce:

Let us be faithful to duty
Let us be unselfish
Let us be loyal
Let us be true to obligations
Let us love one another

And No Garden is Complete Without Turnips:

Turn up for important meetings
Turn up with a smile
Turn up with good ideas
Turn up with determination to make everything count for something good and worthwhile.

BAKED LIMA BEANS

2 c. cooked, dried baby lima beans
¼ c. mild molasses
1 c. dairy sour cream
1 Tbsp. minced onion
½ tsp. dry mustard
⅛ tsp. pepper
1 tsp. salt
1 tsp. Worcestershire sauce
3 slices bacon

Drain beans, saving ½ cup liquid. Combine with molasses, sour cream, onion, mustard, pepper, salt and Worcestershire sauce. Place beans in a 3 quart casserole. Add liquid. Arrange bacon slices on top. Bake in slow oven (325°) for 1 hour. Makes 8 servings.

Rebecca K. Stoltzfus

BARBECUED LIMA BEANS

2 c. lima beans
2 Tbsp. butter
1 medium onion
2 Tbsp. flour
2 Tbsp. brown sugar
1 Tbsp. vinegar
1 c. canned, whole tomatoes
½ c. tomato juice

Fry onion in butter. Add vinegar, sugar and flour. Mix well and add rest of ingredients. Ham or bacon can also be added. Cook limas 5 to 10 minutes. Add to sauce. Bake at 350° for 30 minutes.

Nancy Ann Esch
Naomi Grace Zook

STRING BEAN CASSEROLE

Make layers of canned string beans and onion rings. Add celery or mushroom soup. Top with bread crumbs. Bake at 350° for 1 hour.

Mrs. Edna B. Zook

BAKED BEANS

1 gal. navy beans or Great Northern beans
1 tsp. salt
1 ½ c. tomato juice
¾ c. catsup
dab of mustard (if you wish)
1 c. brown sugar
¾ c. molasses
4 hot dogs or bacon on top

Bake 1 hour at 350°.

Fannie Riehl
Ruth Stoltzfus

OLD SETTLERS BAKED BEANS

½ lb. ground beef
½ lb. bacon, diced
1 medium onion, chopped
⅓ c. sugar
⅓ c. brown sugar
¼ c. ketchup
¼ c. barbecue sauce
1 Tbsp. prepared mustard
½ tsp. pepper
½ tsp. chili powder
1 (16 oz.) can pork and beans, undrained
1 (16 oz.) can kidney beans, rinsed and drained
1 (16 oz.) can Great Northern beans, rinsed and drained

In a large skillet cook beef, bacon and onion until meat is done and onion tender. Drain any fat. Combine all remaining ingredients except beans. Add to meat mixture. Mix well. Stir in beans. Place in a greased 2 ½ quart casserole. Bake, covered, at 350° for 1 hour.

Linda Fisher

COOKED CELERY

2 qt. celery
1 tsp. salt
1 c. water
½ c. sugar
butter (size of a walnut)
2 tsp. vinegar
½ c. milk
2 ½ Tbsp. brown sugar
2 Tbsp. flour

Boil the celery, salt, water, sugar and butter until soft, then add rest of ingredients. Serves 6. Like they have for weddings.

Nancy Ann Esch

MOTHER KING'S CELERY

5 lb. sugar
1 lb. butter (a chunk in each kettle)
8 eggs
1 Tbsp. salt (scant)
2 qt. cream
3 or 4 cans evaporated milk
2 Tbsp. vinegar
flour

You will need 4 or 5 big kettles.

Mix 3 tablespoons flour with 2 tablespoons vinegar and a little water. Beat 2 eggs, then add 1 ½ cups sugar and beat again, then add to flour, cream and evaporated milk. When celery is soft cooked, add this mixture but not while boiling. Let come to a boil to thicken. If not juicy enough, add some milk. If not thick enough, more flour. (I just mix for 1 kettle at a time.) Cook salt, butter, 1 cup sugar with celery. Cook celery with very little water (½ cup). (Keep rusty and hollow stuff out.)

Katie S. King

CARROT PATTIES

1 c. cooked carrots, mashed
2 c. soft bread crumbs
2 beaten eggs
¼ c. chopped onions or less
dash of pepper
1 tsp. salt
½ c. shredded Velveeta cheese
1 Tbsp. snipped parsley (if desired)

Mix together and fry until nice and brown.

Elsie Kauffman

GLAZED CARROTS

6 carrots, cooked
½ c. butter
½ c. sugar

Put carrots in casserole and put in the butter and sugar. Heat in oven.

Barbie Zook

GOURMET POTATOES

6 medium potatoes
1 c. shredded cheese
¼ c. butter
½ c. chopped onions
1 ½ c. sour milk
1 tsp. salt
¼ tsp. pepper
2 Tbsp. butter
1 Tbsp. paprika

Cook potatoes and grate. Combine cheese and butter until melted. Take off heat. Stir in sour cream, salt and pepper. Put into a 2 quart casserole. Dot with butter and paprika. Bake at 350° for 30 minutes (uncovered).

Fannie Glick
Susie S. King

POTATO FILLING

4 c. mashed potatoes
2 Tbsp. minced parsley
2 eggs
4 Tbsp. melted butter
2 qt. bread cubes
½ c. chopped celery
½ tsp. poultry or seasoned salt
½ tsp. pepper
¼ tsp. onion salt
½ c. milk

Mix mashed potatoes with beaten eggs and milk. Soak bread cubes in water and squeeze dry. Add to potato mixture. Stir in other ingredients and mix well. Layer in casserole dish twice with ½ cup butter, ending with butter on top. Bake 1 hour at 325°.

Sylvia Petersheim

POTATO PUFFS

1 c. mashed potatoes
1 or 2 beaten eggs
¼ to ½ c. flour
¼ tsp. salt
1 tsp. baking powder

Drop by teaspoon in deep fat.

Sara Stoltzfus
Linda Fisher

ASPARAGUS AND BREAD DISH

bread
4 eggs
2 c. milk
salt and pepper
onion
2 ½ c. cooked asparagus
cheese

Lay slices of bread in bottom of a 9 x 9-inch pan. Beat eggs with milk, salt, pepper and onion and pour over bread. Bake 25 minutes. Add the asparagus and put sliced cheese on top of asparagus and bake 10 more minutes.

Fannie Glick

BAKED CABBAGE CASSEROLE

1 small head lettuce
2 c. sliced sausage
dash of pepper
2 eggs
1 c. milk
2 c. diced potatoes, cooked
1 tsp. salt
3 Tbsp. butter
4 slices cubed bread

Line a baking dish with cabbage leaves. Cut remaining cabbage in small pieces. Mix eggs, milk and bread cubes and add the rest of the ingredients to it, except butter. Put in cabbage lined dish. Dot with butter. Bake 40 to 45 minutes at 350°.

Mary Stoltzfus

BAKED SWEET POTATOES

4 c. sweet potatoes, peeled and cut
1 tsp. salt
1 c. brown sugar
1 tsp. flour
½ c. cream

Add water to the sweet potatoes and salt and cook until almost tender. Drain. Put the cooked sweet potatoes in a greased casserole and add the brown sugar, flour and cream. Bake at 350° for 20 to 30 minutes or until sticky. Cover top with small marshmallows and brown lightly until they begin to melt.

Edna Zook
Liz Stoltzfus

BAKED SWEET POTATOES

5 medium size sweet potatoes
1 tsp. salt
¾ c. brown sugar
2 Tbsp. butter
3 Tbsp. flour
8 marshmallows
1 c. thin cream

Cook potatoes until tender. Drain and cool off a little. Cut potatoes in half lengthwise and put in baking dish. Mix salt, sugar and flour and pour over potatoes. Dot with butter and marshmallows and pour the cream over top. Bake at 350° for 45 to 50 minutes.

Elsie Kauffman

SWEET POTATO CASSEROLE

3 c. mashed sweet potatoes
2 eggs, beaten
½ c. milk
½ c. sugar
½ tsp. salt
½ stick melted butter
½ tsp. vanilla
½ c. sugar
1 c. finely chopped nuts
⅓ c. flour
⅓ stick butter

Mix together the potatoes, eggs, milk, sugar, salt, melted butter and vanilla and put in casserole. Mix the sugar, nuts, flour and butter and spread over top of potatoes. Bake at 350° for 35 minutes.

Mary Stoltzfus

BAKED CORN

1 ½ pt. creamed or whole kernel corn
2 rounded Tbsp. cornstarch
¾ c. Carnation milk
2 eggs, beaten
¼ c. sugar
1 tsp. salt
½ tsp. pepper

Mix and put in casserole, then pour 3 tablespoons melted butter over top. Bake at 350° for 1 ½ hours.

Katie King
(Hammertown)

BAKED CORN

2 c. corn
1 ½ Tbsp. flour
1 c. milk
½ tsp. pepper
2 eggs
½ c. butter
2 c. bread cubes
sugar (if you wish)

Mix corn, flour, milk, pepper and beaten eggs. Melt butter, then add bread cubes. Pour over top. Bake at 350° for 1 hour.

Sylvia Petersheim
Elizabeth Stoltzfus
Linda Fisher

HOT PINEAPPLE

1 stick butter
1 c. sugar
1 can crushed pineapple
3 eggs, beaten well
5 slices bread, crusts cut off and diced

Cream butter and sugar. Add beaten eggs, pineapple and bread. Grease casserole. Bake 45 minutes at 350°.

Fannie Riehl

HARVARD BEETS

½ c. sugar
½ Tbsp. cornstarch
¼ c. vinegar
¼ c. water
2 c. cooked beets or canned
2 Tbsp. margarine

Mix the sugar and cornstarch. Add vinegar and water. Boil together 5 minutes. Add beets and let stand at least 30 minutes, not on heat. Just before serving, bring to a boil and add margarine.

(Vern) Mary Ann Paul

ONION RINGS

2 large onions, peeled, cut in ¼-inch slices and separated into rings
1 egg
2 tsp. lemon juice
¾ c. water
1 Tbsp. cooking oil
1 c. flour
1 ½ tsp. baking powder
½ tsp. salt

Beat together the egg, lemon juice, water and cooking oil. Add the flour, baking powder and salt. Beat smooth. Heat oil to 375°. Dip onions in batter and fry until golden brown. Turn over once. Drain on paper towels.

Anna Fisher

ZUCCHINI - FRIED

2 c. unpeeled, grated zucchini
½ c. Parmesan cheese
½ c. Bisquick
2 eggs
salt and pepper to taste

Beat eggs and mix with zucchini. Add Bisquick, cheese, salt and pepper. Drop by spoonfuls on hot buttered griddle (medium heat). Cook on each side about 10 minutes.

Louise Utter

ZUCCHINI CASSEROLE

4 c. grated zucchini
1 c. Bisquick
⅓ c. vegetable oil
½ c. or more grated cheese (any kind)
½ tsp. garlic powder
1 Tbsp. parsley flakes
4 eggs

Beat eggs before adding. Browned hamburg or onions may be added, too. Bake at 350° for 45 to 60 minutes.

Katie King
(Hammertown)

ZUCCHINI FRITTERS

½ c. milk
1 egg, beaten
1 c. flour
1 ½ tsp. baking powder
½ or 1 oz. pkg. Ranch style dip mix
2 c. shredded zucchini

Combine milk and egg. Stir together dry ingredients and egg mixture. Blend well. Fold in zucchini. Fry in deep fat. Drop by teaspoonful in deep fat until golden brown.

Mary Ann Smucker

CORN FRITTERS

2 c. corn
1 tsp. salt
¼ tsp. pepper
1 Tbsp. butter
1 egg
¼ c. milk
½ c. flour
1 c. cracker crumbs
1 ¼ tsp. baking powder

Nancy Ann Esch
Priscilla Fisher

RANCH POTATO CASSEROLE

6 to 8 medium potatoes
½ c. sour cream
½ c. Ranch style salad dressing
¼ c. crumbled, fried bacon
2 Tbsp. fresh parsley
1 c. shredded cheese

Topping:

½ c. shredded cheese
2 c. slightly crushed cornflakes
¼ c. butter, melted

Cook potatoes and set aside. Combine sour cream, dressing, parsley and 1 cup cheese. Place potatoes in greased cake pan. Pour sour cream mixture over potatoes and gently toss. Add bacon. Top with ½ cup cheese. Combine cornflakes and butter. Sprinkle over casserole. Bake at 350° for 40 to 45 minutes.

Anna Fisher

Hints for Bread

Baking bread? By letting your bread dough rise in a plastic bag, you can punch it down hard and knead it vigorously, since the dough doesn't dry out.

Loaves will yield a fine texture if the dough is frozen a day or two before baking. Be sure to let them rise before baking.

When baking, use organically raised, stone-ground flour. (We use soya, millet, rye.) But only flour enough as can be used within 4 to 6 weeks and refrigerate in an airtight container. Leave uncovered at room temperature for 2 hours if recipe calls for yeast.

Bread crumbs may be powdered via a coffee grinder or blender and used as a seasoning base. Hard or dried rolls and bread, including heels, offer a good source, so why buy? Separate into two or three portions. To each add a good pinch of a different blend of herbs. My favorites include basil, marjoram, savory, and oregano. Store the crumbs in your freezer.

Need dry bread in a hurry? Place a few slices on your oven rack and warm. The bread will dry out very well and will be quite crisp.

A heated knife blade will cut through fresh bread more easily.

You can often clean wallpaper by rubbing it with soft bread. Try it!

Breads, Rolls & Pastries

Lord, help me to live each day
so that at the end of it there is
nothing I cannot share with you,
nothing for which I cannot give thanks.

Recipe for a Good Housewife

Two tablespoons of common sense,
One spoonful of wit,
Four spoonfuls of patience,
Three spoonfuls of how to sew,
Half spoonful of how to darn.

Mix well before using, so that
You know she has all these qualities.
Be sure to KNOW and don't BELIEVE.
Seeing and experiencing is believing,
And when you have seen, then take her,
And you will have a happy home.

There are men who never, never eat a single piece of pie,
Be it pumpkin, peach or apple, so 'tis said,
No the explanation is simple, when you know the reason why
Like the women who don't gossip they are dead.

BREADS, ROLLS & PASTRIES

GIVE US THIS DAY OUR DAILY BREAD

Man shall not live by bread alone
Our Lord and Master said
But by the Living Word of God
Our souls need be fed.

CRACKERS

8 c. flour
1 c. lard or butter
2 tsp. soda
2 tsp. cream of tartar, mixed with buttermilk

Mix all ingredients and roll fine. Sprinkle with salt. Bake at 325°.

Sara Stoltzfus

CORN MEAL MUFFINS

1 c. corn meal
1 c. all-purpose flour
1 tsp. baking powder
1 tsp. soda
2 Tbsp. sugar
3 Tbsp. shortening
1 egg
1 c. sour milk or buttermilk
½ tsp. salt

Mix together and bake in muffin pan. Bake at 400° for 20 to 25 minutes. Makes 1 dozen.

Elsie Kauffman

APPLE MUFFINS

⅓ c. sugar
4 Tbsp. shortening
3 tsp. baking powder
1 egg
1 ½ c. milk
2 c. flour
1 ½ c. diced apples
¼ tsp. cinnamon

Topping:

3 Tbsp. sugar
¼ tsp. cinnamon
¼ tsp. nutmeg

Bake at 350°.

Barbara Zook

BLUEBERRY MUFFINS

1 ½ c. all-purpose flour
2 tsp. baking powder
pinch of salt
½ stick oleo
½ c. sugar
1 egg
1 tsp. vanilla
½ c. milk
1 ½ c. blueberries

Topping:

2 Tbsp. butter
2 Tbsp. brown sugar
¼ tsp. cinnamon
¼ c. chopped nuts

Sift flour, baking powder and salt onto wax paper. In larger bowl cream oleo and sugar until fluffy. Beat in egg and vanilla. Stir in flour alternately with milk. Fold in blueberries and bake in muffin pans for 20 minutes at 375°. Put topping ingredients in pan and melt. Put topping on each muffin.

Helen Miller

BLUEBERRY MUFFINS

2 Tbsp. butter
⅔ c. sugar
½ c. milk
1 egg
⅛ tsp. salt
1 ½ c. flour
1 tsp. baking powder
1 c. blueberries

Cream butter, sugar and egg. Add milk. Add dry ingredients. Fold in blueberries. Sprinkle a bit of sugar on top. Bake at 350° about 30 minutes.

Linda Fisher

BISCUITS

1 c. sourdough
1 c. flour
¾ tsp. baking soda
¼ tsp. salt
⅓ c. margarine or oil

Mix well. Drop by teaspoon on greased cookie sheet or muffin tin. Bake at 350° for 10 to 20 minutes.

(Vern) Mary Ann Paul

DIANE'S CORNMEAL MUSH

1 c. cornmeal
1 c. cold water
3 c. boiling water
1 tsp. salt
2 Tbsp. margarine
flour

Grease loaf pan. Mix cornmeal and cold water in saucepan. Stir in boiling water and salt. Cook, stirring constantly, until mixture thickens and boils. Cover and cook over low heat for 10 minutes. Spoon into pans. Cover and chill at least 12 hours. Invert pan to unmold cornmeal. Cut loaf into ½-inch slices. Melt margarine in large skillet. Coat slices with flour and brown in skillet. Makes 9 servings.

(Vern) Mary Ann Paul

FRENCH TOAST

3 beaten eggs
9 oz. milk

Add milk to beaten eggs. Dip pieces of bread into the mixture. Melt and lightly brown butter in a pan. Place in bread pieces and sprinkle with salt. Fry until golden brown on both sides. Serve with syrup.

Susie King

STICKY BUNS

2 c. mashed potatoes, without milk
1 c. potato water
3 eggs, beaten
1 c. sugar
1 c. vegetable oil
3 pkg. yeast, dissolved in ¾ c. warm water
1 tsp. salt
about 5 lb. flour

Mix together eggs, sugar, salt, oil, potatoes and potato water. Add yeast and mix well. Stir in just enough flour so that dough can be handled. Roll out dough. Spread soft butter on dough. Sprinkle brown sugar and cinnamon on top. Roll up dough. Cut into pieces.

Topping:

1 c. butter
2 c. brown sugar
¾ c. water

Bring to a boil and put in pans, then add buns.
Variation: Instead of batter topping, frost with white icing.

Linda Fisher
Priscilla King

CREAM STICKS OR DOUGHNUTS

2 Tbsp. yeast, dissolved in 1 c. warm water
1 c. scalded milk
½ c. margarine
⅔ c. sugar
2 eggs
½ tsp. salt
1 tsp. vanilla
6 c. flour or more (just so it isn't too sticky)

Let dough rise until double in size. Knead and form into sticks or doughnuts.

Naomi King

CINNAMON BUNS

1 c. scalded milk
¼ c. lukewarm water
1 tsp. salt
¼ c. lard
¼ c. sugar
2 well beaten eggs
1 Tbsp. yeast
3 ½ c. flour

Naomi Petersheim

BUTTERMILK BISCUITS

2 c. flour
2 tsp. baking powder
1 tsp. sugar
1 tsp. baking soda
5 Tbsp. butter
¾ c. buttermilk

Mix flour, sugar, baking powder, salt and soda as for pie crumbs. Cut in butter. Make a well in the center. Add buttermilk, stirring lightly. Place on cookie sheet. Bake in preheated oven at 450° for 10 to 12 minutes. Eat warm with butter and honey or jelly.

Rachel Esh

MONKEY BREAD

2 cans biscuits, roll into balls (Pillsbury)
½ c. white sugar
1 tsp. cinnamon
½ stick butter
¾ c. brown sugar

Put balls of biscuits in greased pan. Bring the butter and brown sugar to a boil and pour over the buns. Bake at 300° about 20 minutes. Put nuts on, if you want to.

Rachel King

POTATO BUNS

5 eggs
1 c. lard, lukewarm
2 c. mashed potatoes
2 c. lukewarm water
1 c. sugar
1 Tbsp. salt
2 Tbsp. yeast
12 c. flour

Put yeast in warm water for 10 or 15 minutes. Work ingredients well and let rise until light. Roll out and cut. Put in pan. Let rise again. Bake 20 minutes at 325°.

Mrs. Elam Z. Stoltzfus

POTATO ROLLS

2 Tbsp. yeast with 2 c. lukewarm water
2 c. hot mashed potatoes
1 c. Wesson oil
1 c. sugar
1 tsp. salt
5 eggs

Let the yeast and water stand for 15 minutes. Do not stir. Mix the mashed potatoes with the oil and stir until smooth. Add the sugar, salt and eggs. Mix well. Add yeast mixture. Add 9 cups flour or more if sticky. Let rise 1 hour. Form in flat ball on cookie sheets. Let rise 1 hour. Bake 10 minutes at 350°.

Barbara Zook
Priscilla King

RAISIN BREAD

½ c. sugar
2 Tbsp. salt
½ c. lard or oil
1 ½ c. hot milk
2 eggs, beaten
flour
2 Tbsp. yeast, dissolved in 1 c. warm water
1 Tbsp. cinnamon
1 box raisins

Add enough flour to mixture to make a soft dough and not sticky anymore. Cook the raisins 5 minutes in water to cover. Cool and drain. Put half of flour in before adding raisins. You should have about 4 ½ to 5 cups of liquid. Less raisins can be used. Makes 4 or 5 loaves.

Elizabeth Stoltzfus
Rachel Esh

BUBBLE BREAD

bread dough, enough for 2 loaves
1 c. sugar
2 tsp. cinnamon
1 stick margarine
nuts, chopped fine

Grease an angel food cake pan. Pinch off dough the size of walnuts or smaller. Roll in melted butter, then in sugar and cinnamon mixture. Place in cake pan in layers and sprinkle each layer with nuts. Pour leftover butter and sugar mixture over top. Let rise until double in size. Bake at 325° for 45 minutes.

Rachel Esh

BEST EVER BANANA BREAD

1 ¾ c. flour
1 ½ c. sugar
1 tsp. baking soda
½ tsp. salt
2 eggs
2 ripe medium bananas, mashed (1 c.)
½ c. vegetable oil
¼ c. plus 1 Tbsp. buttermilk
1 tsp. vanilla
1 c. chopped walnuts

In a large bowl stir together flour, sugar, soda and salt. In another bowl combine eggs, bananas, oil, buttermilk and vanilla. Add to flour mixture, stirring just until combined. Fold in nuts. Pour into a greased loaf pan. Bake at 325° for 1 hour and 20 minutes. Yields 1 loaf. Recipe does not double well.

Linda Fisher

ZUCCHINI BREAD

3 c. flour
1 tsp. baking soda
¼ tsp. baking powder
1 ½ tsp. cinnamon
1 tsp. salt
2 c. sugar
3 eggs
1 c. oil
2 c. grated zucchini
½ c. chopped nuts
1 tsp. flour

Mix the flour, baking soda, baking powder, cinnamon and salt and set aside. Combine the sugar, eggs and oil. Mix the nuts with the flour, if desired. Combine all with the zucchini and nuts. Bake 45 minutes at 350°. Makes 2 small loaves.

Mrs. Elam Z. Stoltzfus
Anna King
Mary Stoltzfus
Helen Miller

PUMPKIN BREAD

1 c. Wesson oil
3 c. white sugar
4 eggs
2 c. pumpkin (pulp)
⅔ c. water
3 ½ c. sifted flour (Gold Medal)
2 tsp. soda
1 tsp. nutmeg
1 ½ tsp. salt
1 tsp. cinnamon

Add nuts or raisins, if desired. Bake at 350° for 40 to 45 minutes. Makes 3 loaves.

Katie King
(Hammertown)

PINEAPPLE ZUCCHINI BREAD

3 eggs
2 c. sugar
2 tsp. vanilla
1 c. oil
2 c. zucchini, grated and peeled
3 ½ c. flour
1 c. crushed pineapple, well drained
1 ½ tsp. salt
1 ½ tsp. baking soda
¾ tsp. baking powder

Mix eggs, sugar, vanilla and oil. Blend until light. Add zucchini and dry ingredients alternating with pineapple. Bake in well-greased and floured bread pans. Bake 1 hour or until done at 325°. Makes 2 loaves.

Barbara King

WHOLE WHEAT BREAD

4 c. warm water
2 rounded Tbsp. yeast
1 ½ Tbsp. salt
1 Tbsp. vinegar
¾ c. honey
2 c. whole wheat flour
10 c. bread flour
4 Tbsp. melted lard

Mix all together and knead. If too sticky, add a little more flour and dip hands into melted lard to knead. Let rise. Knead down. Let rise again, then put into bread pans. Let rise until a little higher than pans. Bake in a 350° oven for 30 minutes. Makes 4 loaves.

Elsie Kauffman

100% WHOLE WHEAT BREAD

1 Tbsp. yeast, dissolved in ½ c. warm water and 1 tsp. honey
¾ c. honey
1 Tbsp. vinegar
2 Tbsp. blackstrap molasses
2 Tbsp. liquid lecithin
2 eggs
1 Tbsp. salt
10 ½ to 11 c. whole wheat flour

Mix together first 6 ingredients and 2 cups flour. Add yeast mixture, then rest of flour. Work in 2 tablespoons oil, then work well every 20 minutes using a small amount of oil each time.

Fannie Glick

BREAD

½ c. sugar
2 Tbsp. salt
2 Tbsp. yeast
3 c. water
4 Tbsp. lard
1 Tbsp. blackstrap molasses
6 ¾ c. flour

Mix all together. Let rise until double. Punch down. Let rise double again, then shape in 3 loaves. Let rise until double. Bake at 350° for 25 to 30 minutes.

Mrs. Edna B. Zook

BREAD

2 Tbsp. yeast, in 1 c. warm water
2 Tbsp. sugar
4 Tbsp. Karo
4 Tbsp. Wesson oil
½ Tbsp. sugar
pinch of salt
2 c. hot water
8 or 9 c. bread flour

Add sugar to the yeast and warm water. Let stand until it foams. Mix the Karo, oil, sugar, pinch of salt and hot water. Mix yeast mixture and add flour. Mix all together and let rise until double. Punch down. Let rise again, then shape in 1 pound loaves. Let rise until double. Bake at 350° for 25 to 30 minutes.

Susie S. King
Priscilla King

WHITE BREAD

½ c. sugar
3 Tbsp. salt
3 Tbsp. lard
4 c. hot water
1 Tbsp. sugar
2 heaping Tbsp. yeast
3 c. lukewarm water
16 c. flour (more or less)

Dissolve the ½ cup sugar, salt and lard in 4 cups hot water. Dissolve the 1 tablespoon sugar and yeast in 3 cups lukewarm water and add to first mixture. Stir in 10 cups flour and beat well. Add remaining flour, beating well after every 2 cups. Takes about 16 cups flour all together (a little more or less). Let rise 10 minutes. Knead down and let rise 15 to 20 minutes. Knead down and let rise until double in size (about 1 hour). Put in pans and let rise until it comes to top of pans (about 1 hour). Bake at 350° for 25 to 30 minutes. Makes 8 loaves.

Katie King
(Hammertown)

WHITE BREAD

4 c. warm water
2 Tbsp. yeast
5 Tbsp. sugar
1 Tbsp. salt
2 Tbsp. lard (heaping)
3 Tbsp. Wesson oil
10 c. white flour
1 to 2 c. whole wheat flour

Dissolve yeast in water. Add all ingredients except oil. Knead thoroughly. Let rise until double in bulk. Punch down and add oil. Let rise again. Punch down and divide into 1 pound loaves. Put into greased pans and let rise until a little above pans. Bake at 350° for 30 minutes.

Nancy Ann Esch

BREAD

2 Tbsp. yeast, in 1 c. water and 1 tsp. sugar
¾ c. oil
½ c. sugar
1 Tbsp. salt
4 c. lukewarm water

Dissolve the yeast in the water and sugar. In bowl put the oil, ½ cup sugar, salt and rest of the water. Last add the yeast mixture. Put in flour until somewhat sticky, beating well. Let rise. Punch down and turn. Let rise again. Add a little oil to work. Bake at 375°. Makes 6 loaves.

Naomi King

WHITE BREAD

4 c. warm water
2 Tbsp. yeast
5 Tbsp. sugar
1 Tbsp. salt
2 Tbsp. lard (heaping)
3 Tbsp. Wesson oil
10 c. white flour
1 to 2 c. whole wheat flour

Dissolve yeast in water. Add all ingredients except oil. Knead thoroughly. Let rise until double in bulk. Punch down and add oil. Let rise again. Punch down and divide into 1 pound loaves. Put into greased pans and let rise until a little above pans. Bake at 350° for 30 minutes.

Nancy Ann Esch

BREAD

3 c. water
1 pkg. yeast
3 Tbsp. sugar
1 Tbsp. salt
3 Tbsp. vegetable oil
flour

Dissolve yeast in 3 cups warm water. Add rest of ingredients. Add enough flour to make a soft dough. Let rise 1 hour. Work well. Let rise 1 ½ hours. Put in pans. Let rise 2 hours. Bake at 350° for 30 minutes.

Linda Fisher

BREAD

1 qt. plus 1 ⅓ c. water
⅔ c. sugar
2 Tbsp. salt
2 pkg. yeast
4 Tbsp. melted Crisco
flour

Put sugar and salt in bowl. Add lukewarm water and yeast. Let stand 5 minutes or so. Add Crisco and mix well, then flour to make a soft dough, just so it doesn't stick to hands. Let stand ½ hour, then knead real well again. After that, knead it down several times, 4 hours from time put yeast in water. Put dough in pans. Grease and prick evenly with fork. Bake 15 minutes at 425°, then turn it back to 350° for another 15 minutes.

Anna King

FOUNDATION SWEET DOUGH RECIPE

1 c. scalded milk
1 c. lukewarm water
2 cakes compressed yeast
½ c. shortening
½ c. sugar
1 ½ tsp. salt
2 eggs, beaten
6 c. flour
½ tsp. nutmeg or ½ lemon rind or juice may be added

Scald milk and pour it over sugar, salt and shortening. Dissolve yeast in lukewarm water. Add beaten eggs. When milk has cooled to lukewarm temperature, add the yeast and beaten eggs. Beat well. Add flour gradually, beating well. Knead lightly, working in just enough flour so that dough can be handled. Place dough in a greased bowl. Cover and let stand in a warm place. Let rise until double in bulk (about 2 hours). Use this to make cinnamon rolls.

Sylvia Stoltzfus

CINNAMON ROLLS

1 recipe Foundation Sweet Dough (preceding recipe)
6 Tbsp. melted butter
1 ½ c. brown sugar
1 Tbsp. cinnamon
1 c. raisins (optional)

When dough is light, divide into 2 portions. Roll into oblong pieces ¼-inch thick. Brush with melted butter and sprinkle with brown sugar and raisins. Roll like a jelly roll and cut slices ½-inch thick, using a sharp knife. Place slices 1-inch apart on greased tin with cut side down. Let rise in warm place until light (about 1 hour). Bake at 400° for 20 to 25 minutes.

Sylvia Stoltzfus

CINNAMON ROLLS

Dough:

1 c. milk, scalded
2 Tbsp. shortening
2 Tbsp. sugar
1 tsp. salt
1 yeast cake
¼ c. lukewarm water
1 beaten egg
3 ½ c. flour

Blend Together:

½ c. brown sugar
½ c. shortening
2 Tbsp. white Karo
2 tsp. cinnamon

Put this mixture in bottom of pan. Set the rolls on top and bake. Turn out of pan with bottom side up.

Combine milk, shortening, sugar and salt. Cool to lukewarm. Add yeast cake, softened in lukewarm water and egg. Gradually stir in flour to form a soft dough. Beat vigorously. Cover and let rise in warm place until double in bulk, about 2 hours. Knead down and roll out. Spread the top with butter and sprinkle with brown sugar and cinnamon. Roll and cut as for a jelly roll.

Anna King

SWEET DOUGH BUNS

½ c. lukewarm water
½ Tbsp. sugar
1 Tbsp. yeast
3 Tbsp. shortening
¼ c. sugar
½ Tbsp. salt
2 eggs, beaten
3 ½ to 4 c. flour

Mix the lukewarm water, ½ tablespoon sugar and yeast and let stand until dissolved. Combine the shortening, ¼ cup sugar, salt and eggs and mix with the yeast mixture and add the flour. Let rise until double in size. Work down and divide into 2 parts. Roll each part to about ½-inch thick. Sprinkle on cinnamon and raisins. Roll up and cut into 1 ½-inch pieces. Put into greased pan. Let rise 1 to 1 ½ hours. Bake at 350° for 15 to 20 minutes.

Fannie Riehl

SOFT PRETZELS

1 pkg. yeast
⅛ c. warm water
1 ⅓ c. warm water
⅓ c. brown sugar
5 c. bread flour
coarse salt for tops

Dissolve yeast in ⅛ cup warm water. Stir in rest of ingredients. Knead until dough is smooth and elastic. Shape into pretzels. Bring 2 tablespoons soda to each cup of water to a boil. Place pretzels into boiling water for 30 seconds. Remove and place on a heavily buttered cookie sheet. Salt top of pretzels. Bake in a preheated 550° oven until brown. Brush tops with melted butter.

Aarianne Petersheim
Sylvia Petersheim
Linda Fisher

SOFT PRETZELS

1 ½ c. water
2 heaping Tbsp. yeast
½ tsp. salt
4 c. flour
⅓ c. honey or brown sugar

Let rise 10 minutes. Shape. Dip in 1 tablespoon soda mixed with ½ cup warm water. Sprinkle with salt. Bake at 550° until brown. Butter them.

Elsie Kauffman

SOFT PRETZELS

3 Tbsp. yeast
dash of salt
2 Tbsp. brown sugar
3 c. warm water
8 c. flour

Let the yeast, salt, sugar and warm water stand for 10 minutes, then add the flour.

Anna King

MONKEY BUNS

2 cans biscuits, cut in half
½ c. sugar
1 tsp. cinnamon
½ stick margarine
¾ c. brown sugar
2 Tbsp. water

Roll biscuits in sugar and cinnamon mixture and put in greased cookie pan. Mix the margarine, brown sugar and water. Bring to a boil and pour over biscuits. Bake 20 minutes. Delicious for quick snack!

Nancy Ann Esch
Aarianne Petersheim

STICKY BUNS

2 pkg. yeast
1 c. warm water
1 Tbsp. sugar (white)
1 c. water
½ c. shortening, part butter, melted
⅔ c. white sugar
1 ½ tsp. salt
2 eggs
a little vanilla
4 c. all-purpose flour
4 c. bread flour

Mix the yeast with 1 cup warm water and let stand 5 minutes. Combine all ingredients. Put molasses in greased pan, some butter and 2 cups brown sugar. Wet with Pet milk and spread on dough when rolled out.

Rachel King

DOUGHNUTS

2 tsp. sugar, dissolved in ½ c. warm water
1 yeast cake
1 c. scalded milk
2 tsp. salt
1 c. sugar
2 ¼ c. flour, sifted
4 eggs
1 c. hot mashed potatoes
1 c. melted shortening
5 c. flour or more

Add yeast to the sugar and water mixture in a large bowl. Combine the scalded milk, salt and sugar. Let it cool, then add yeast solution to milk solution. Blend in 2 ¼ cups flour, sifted. Let it stand 1 hour, then add eggs, potatoes and shortening. Add 5 cups of flour or more. Mix well, then raise again. Roll and cut them. Put in warm place to rise again. Fry in deep fat.

(Vern) Mary Ann Paul

SOUR MILK DOUGHNUTS

1 c. sugar
2 eggs
1 Tbsp. sour cream
1 c. sour milk
½ tsp. baking soda
½ tsp. salt
½ tsp. cinnamon
½ tsp. nutmeg
flour, as needed
¼ c. melted margarine

Mix sugar, butter, eggs, milk, soda, salt, spices and 1 cup flour. When the doughnuts cool, roll in powdered sugar.

(Vern) Mary Ann Paul

CINNAMON BUNS

2 eggs, beaten well
1 yeast cake, dissolved in 1 c. warm water
½ c. sugar
1 tsp. salt
2 Tbsp. butter or margarine, melted
4 c. flour

Mix and let stand 5 or 6 hours. Knead and roll flat. Melt butter enough to cover the dough. Sprinkle with cinnamon, brown sugar and raisins to taste. Roll it up and cut in slices about 2-inches thick. Put in bottom of pan:

1 c. brown sugar
¾ c. butter
2 Tbsp. Karo

Stir it up in the pan, then put dough on the mixture. Let stand 1 hour. Bake at 350° until golden brown.

(Vern) Mary Ann Paul

WAFFLES

2 c. flour
2 tsp. baking powder
5 Tbsp. butter
¼ tsp. salt
3 eggs
1 ½ c. milk

Sift flour, then measure. Add other dry ingredients. Sift 3 times. To the well beaten egg yolks, add flour mixture with milk. Add butter which has been melted. Fold in egg whites and bake in waffle iron.

Naomi Petersheim

FEATHER PANCAKES

1 c. flour
2 Tbsp. sugar
2 Tbsp. baking powder
1 tsp. salt
1 egg
1 c. milk
2 Tbsp. cooking oil

Stir together flour, sugar, baking powder and salt. Combine egg, milk and oil. Add all at once to dry ingredients, beating until blended. Makes 8 (4-inch) pancakes.

Naomi Grace Zook

WHOLE WHEAT PANCAKES

¾ c. whole wheat flour
1 Tbsp. sugar
1 tsp. baking powder
½ tsp. soda
1 c. milk
½ tsp. salt
1 egg
2 Tbsp. oil

421792

Measure and sift dry ingredients. Add egg, milk and oil. Bake on a hot griddle.

Fannie Glick

PANCAKES

1 tsp. sugar
1 tsp. salt
1 Tbsp. shortening
2 egg yolks
2 c. milk
2 c. flour
3 tsp. baking powder
2 egg whites

Measure and sift the dry ingredients together. Add the milk gradually, beating to make a smooth batter. Add the beaten egg yolks and the melted fat. Fold in stiffly beaten egg whites. Bake on a hot griddle. Makes 8 medium size cakes.

Naomi Petersheim
Sylvia Stoltzfus

SILVER SEAL PANCAKES

2 c. flour
2 tsp. baking powder
1 tsp. salt
1 ½ c. milk
3 Tbsp. sugar
2 eggs
2 tsp. butter

Aarianne Petersheim

PANCAKES

2 c. flour
2 tsp. baking powder
1 tsp. salt
2 Tbsp. melted butter
3 Tbsp. sugar
2 eggs, separated
1 c. milk

Beat egg yolks and add milk. Add sifted dry ingredients. Beat thoroughly, then add melted butter. Beat egg whites until light and fluffy and fold into batter. Makes about 10 pancakes.

Nancy Esch
Elizabeth Stoltzfus

MAPLE FLAVORED PANCAKE SYRUP

4 c. sugar
½ c. brown sugar
2 c. water
1 tsp. vanilla
1 tsp. maple flavoring
2 Tbsp. white corn syrup
1 tsp. vinegar

Combine sugar, corn syrup and water. Stir until dissolved. Bring to a boil. Cover, then boil gently for 10 minutes. Remove from heat and cool slightly and add rest of ingredients. Stir only until mixed. Store in refrigerator.

Nancy Esch

PANCAKE AND WAFFLE SYRUP

½ c. brown sugar
4 c. white sugar
2 c. water
1 tsp. vanilla
1 tsp. maple extract

Boil the sugars and water gently for 10 minutes. Add the vanilla and maple extract.

Naomi Petersheim

GRAPE-NUTS

20 c. whole wheat flour
10 c. brown sugar
2 Tbsp. soda
10 c. buttermilk (thick or sour)
1 Tbsp. salt
2 tsp. vanilla
2 tsp. maple flavoring
1 ½ c. margarine or butter

Mix dry ingredients in a bowl. Add soda to buttermilk and mix into dry ingredients. Add melted butter and flavoring last. Bake at 350° until done. Grind and dry until crisp.

Linda Fisher

WHOLE WHEAT GRAPE-NUTS

¾ c. coconut
1 ½ c. cornmeal and enough graham flour to make 3 ½ lb.
¾ c. blackstrap molasses, fill up to 2 c. with Honeybrook molasses
1 c. honey
1 ½ qt. buttermilk
3 heaping tsp. soda

Fannie Glick

GRAHAM CEREAL

1 c. brown sugar
1 c. graham flour
2 c. oatmeal
1 tsp. soda
1 tsp. vanilla
½ tsp. cinnamon
⅓ c. oil
1 c. milk

Bake like cookies or in cake pan, if you wish at 350°.

Fannie Glick

BREAKFAST GRANOLA

10 c. oatmeal
2 c. wheat germ
2 c. brown sugar
1 c. coconut
2 c. crushed cashews
2 c. powdered milk
¾ c. butter
1 c. honey
1 tsp. salt
1 tsp. cinnamon
1 tsp. vanilla
chopped dates or raisins (if desired)

Combine oatmeal, wheat germ, brown sugar and powdered milk. Mix well. Melt butter. Add honey, salt, vanilla and cinnamon. Pour over oatmeal mixture and mix very well. Spread on cookie sheets and roast at 275° for 30 minutes. Stir a couple of times while roasting. Remove from oven and add coconut, raisins and cashews. Cool and store in tight container.

Fannie Glick

GRANOLA CEREAL

10 c. oatmeal
2 c. wheat germ (optional)
2 c. brown sugar
2 Tbsp. molasses or honey
1 c. butter
2 tsp. vanilla

Melt butter. Add molasses, sugar and vanilla. Add remaining ingredients and stir well. Bake in slow oven until golden brown, approximately 2 hours. Stir once while baking. If desired, add nuts, raisins or coconut when cooled.

Ruth Stoltzfus

GRANOLA CEREAL

2 sticks butter or margarine
2 c. brown sugar
½ c. honey or molasses
2 Tbsp. vanilla
12 c. oatmeal
2 c. raisins

Melt the butter or margarine. Add the remaining ingredients. Put in cake pans and bake at 250° for 1 hour, stirring occasionally. Store in an airtight container.

Nancy Esch

ANGEL FOOD

Take a cup of kindness
Mix it well with love
Add a lot of patience
And faith in God above
Sprinkle very generously
with joy and thanks and cheer
And you'll have lots of "Angel Food"
To feast on all the year.

Rachel Esh

FAMILY PIE

One handful of forgiveness
One heaping cupful of love
One pound of unselfishness

Mix together smoothly with complete faith in God.
Add 2 cups of wisdom
One cup of good nature flavor
Sprinkle generously with thoughtfulness
This make a wonderful family pie
One complete pie will serve any size family.

PUMPKIN PIES

2 c. sugar
2 Tbsp. flour
1 tsp. vanilla
sprinkle of cinnamon
2 c. pumpkin
4 egg yolks (beat egg whites until stiff)
2 c. milk, bring to near boil and add last

Bake at 375° for 10 minutes, then at 350° for 35 minutes. Can add 1 teaspoon nutmeg and 1 teaspoon salt, if you wish.

Liz Stoltzfus
Sylvia Stoltzfus

PUMPKIN PIE

1 c. pumpkin
1 c. sugar
2 Tbsp. flour
2 eggs, separated
2 c. milk

Brown butter. Put egg whites in last. Sprinkle with cinnamon. Bake at 450° for 10 minutes, then 350° until done.

Barbie Zook

PUMPKIN PIE

½ c. pumpkin
1 c. brown sugar
½ c. granulated sugar
½ c. molasses
2 Tbsp. flour
¼ tsp. cinnamon
2 c. milk
2 eggs, separated

Beat egg whites until stiff. Fold in last. Bake 10 minutes at 325°, then 30 minutes at 300°.

Katie S. King
Priscilla King

PUMPKIN PIE

1 c. pumpkin
½ c. granulated sugar
½ c. brown sugar
3 eggs, separated
2 Tbsp. flour
1 tsp. cinnamon
1 tsp. nutmeg
2 Tbsp. molasses

Measure pumpkin in bowl. Whip in egg yolk. Add sugars, flour, cinnamon and nutmeg. Add molasses and scalded milk. Add beaten egg whites. Sprinkle top with cinnamon. Bake at 425° for 15 minutes, then 350° for 15 minutes, then at 325° for 15 minutes.

Susie Smucker
Elizabeth Stoltzfus

4 PUMPKIN PIES (NEVER FAIL)

1 ⅔ c. pumpkin
6 egg yolks
3 scant c. sugar
3 Tbsp. flour
1 tsp. salt
6 c. milk

For a smoother pie, add 1 can Pet milk. Last of all, beaten egg whites. Pour into unbaked crusts. Bake 20 minutes at 400°, then 25 minutes at 350°.

Fannie Glick

PUMPKIN PIE

3 c. cooked pumpkin
2 c. sugar
3 eggs
½ tsp. salt
1 tsp. cinnamon
1 tsp. nutmeg
3 Tbsp. flour
1 ½ c. milk

Separate the eggs and beat the yolks into pumpkin. Beat the whites separately and stir in just before filling pie crust. Bake at 350° until done.

(Vern) Mary Ann Paul

STRAWBERRY PIE

1 qt. crushed strawberries
3 c. sugar
¾ c. instant clear jell

Mix sugar and instant clear jell together well. Add the crushed strawberries. Put 1 cup of strawberry mixture in bottom of baked pie crust or graham cracker crust. Add fresh strawberries, cut in half, until full. Add rest of crushed strawberry mixture. Top with Cool Whip.

Barbara King

DELUXE STRAWBERRY PIE

4 c. fresh strawberries, washed and capped
3 Tbsp. cornstarch
1 c. sugar
½ tsp. baking powder
3 drops red food coloring
1 baked 9-inch pie shell

Spread 2 cups berries over bottom of pie shell. Mash or break remaining berries in pan. Add sugar, cornstarch and baking powder and mix well. Place over low heat. Bring to a boil, stirring constantly. Reduce heat and cool 10 minutes. Add food coloring to deepen red mixture. Cool, then pour over raw berries in pie shell. Refrigerate until thoroughly chilled. Top with whipped cream. "Delicious."

Barbie Zook
Mrs. Elam Z. Stoltzfus

APPLE CREAM PIE

3 c. finely cut apple
1 c. brown sugar
1 c. cream
¼ tsp. salt
1 rounded Tbsp. flour

Mix together and put in unbaked pie shell. Bake in hot oven at 450° for 15 minutes, then reduce heat to 325° and bake 30 to 40 minutes longer. When pie is about half done, take a knife and push top apples down to soften. Sprinkle top with cinnamon. Garnish with Cool Whip.

Naomi King

APPLE CRUMB PIE

2 ½ Tbsp. Minute tapioca
¾ c. sugar
¼ tsp. salt
4 c. sliced apples

Crumb Topping:

⅓ c. brown sugar, packed
¼ c. flour or a little more
½ tsp. cinnamon
2 ½ Tbsp. soft butter

Mix the tapioca, sugar, salt and apples and let stand 5 minutes. Mix crumb topping and put on top of apples. Bake at 425° for 45 to 50 minutes. Makes 1 (9-inch) pie. Can also use peaches.

Rachel Esh

DELICIOUS MOST UNUSUAL APPLE PIE

1 c. unsifted flour
1 tsp. baking powder
¾ c. sugar
pinch of salt
½ c. butter
1 egg, beaten
5 sliced apples
½ c. brown sugar, divided
½ tsp. cinnamon

Mix together flour, baking powder, sugar and salt. Add butter and egg. Mix with fork (will be thick like paste). Put apples in square baking dish. Add a little brown sugar. Put big spoonfuls of mixture over apples. Sprinkle with brown sugar and cinnamon. Bake at 325° for 40 minutes or until dough is brown. Serve with whipped cream or ice cream.

Susie King

HUTSULE PIE

2 c. apples
½ c. brown sugar
½ c. granulated sugar
1 tsp. (level) flour
½ c. cream or Pet milk

Mix in bowl. Put in pie crusts. Dot with butter and sprinkle with cinnamon.

Susie S. King

RAISIN CUSTARD PIE

1 ½ c. raisins
1 c. water
¼ c. butter
2 c. granulated sugar
½ tsp. cinnamon
¾ Tbsp. vinegar
5 egg yolks

Cook the raisins, water and butter for 5 minutes. Mix together the sugar, cinnamon, vinegar and egg yolks. Beat egg whites and add last. Mix all together and put in unbaked pie shells. Bake at 400° for 10 minutes, then at 350° for 20 minutes. Makes 2 (8-inch) pies.

Linda Fisher
Fannie Riehl

RAISIN PIE

8 c. water
2 c. raisins
pinch of salt
1 ½ c. white sugar
clear jell

Crumbs:

1 c. flour
½ c. brown sugar
¼ c. shortening
½ tsp. soda
½ tsp. baking powder

Cook the water, raisins and pinch of salt for 1 hour and add the sugar and thicken with clear jell. Pour into pie shells and top with crumbs.

Triple the crumb recipe for the pie.

Aarianne Petersheim

FILLED RAISIN PIE

2 c. raisins
4 Tbsp. flour
2 c. sugar
2 eggs
2 c. water
1 tsp. vinegar
1 tsp. salt

Stew raisins until soft. Add flour, sugar, egg yolks, water, vinegar and salt. Let come to a boil and keep stirring. Cool and pour into baked crust. Top with meringue.

Edna Zook

PECAN PIES

9 Tbsp. butter
2 c. brown sugar
a few grains salt
2 ¼ c. light corn syrup
1 ½ c. milk
9 eggs
2 ¼ tsp. vanilla
1 ½ c. chopped pecans

Cream butter slowly. Beat in sugar and salt. Add eggs one at a time. Beat briskly. Blend entire mixture. Bake 10 minutes at 450°. Reduce heat to 350° and bake until custard sets, about 30 minutes. Makes 3 (9-inch) pies.

Rachel Esh

SOUTHERN PECAN PIE

3 eggs
⅔ c. sugar
1 c. dark corn syrup
⅓ c. melted butter
1 c. pecan halves
1 (9-inch) unbaked pastry shell

Beat eggs thoroughly with sugar, dash of salt, corn syrup and melted butter. Add pecans. Pour in unbaked pastry shell. Bake at 350° for 50 minutes.

Mrs. Susie Smucker

LEMON PIE

1 pkg. lemon pie filling
1 c. sugar
1 Tbsp. clear jell
3 eggs
1 Tbsp. butter
4 c. boiling water

Mix in saucepan and cook until thick. Pour in baked pie shell. Makes 2.

Aarianne Petersheim

LEMON SPONGE PIE

4 Tbsp. butter or margarine
3 ½ c. sugar
rind and juice of 3 lemons
6 c. milk, scalded or 4 ½ c. water
9 eggs, separated
9 Tbsp. flour
pinch of salt

Mix egg yolks with sugar, flour and salt. Add lemon juice, rind, butter and milk. Fold in stiffly beaten egg whites last. Put in unbaked pie shell. Bake at 425° for 15 minutes, then reduce heat to 325° until done. Makes 4 large pies.

Naomi Petersheim
Sylvia Stoltzfus

LEMON SPONGE PIE

1 c. sugar
1 Tbsp. butter
2 eggs
juice of 1 lemon
1 heaping Tbsp. flour
1 c. milk

Mix together sugar, butter, yolk of eggs, lemon juice and flour. Add milk a little at a time so won't curdle with lemon juice. Add beaten egg whites. Bake in low oven.

Mrs. Edna B. Zook

LEMON SPONGE PIE

2 c. granulated sugar
1 grated lemon
2 Tbsp. melted butter
4 Tbsp. flour
4 eggs, beaten separately
2 ½ c. milk

Mix sugar and flour and add melted butter, lemon and milk. Add eggs whites last, beat stiff. Bake at 350°.

Katie S. King
Anna King
Susie King

FRENCH RHUBARB PIE

1 egg
1 c. sugar
1 tsp. vanilla
2 c. diced rhubarb
1 Tbsp. flour

Topping:

¾ c. flour
½ c. brown sugar
⅓ c. butter

Mix together the egg, sugar, vanilla, rhubarb and flour. Put rhubarb mixture into unbaked pie shell. Melt butter and mix with flour and sugar and cover rhubarb mixture. Bake at 400° for 10 minutes. Continue baking at 350° for 30 minutes or until done.

Nancy Ann Esch
Mary Ann Smucker
Elizabeth Stoltzfus

RHUBARB PIE

2 c. rhubarb
1 c. brown sugar
egg yolk
1 Tbsp. flour
a little water

Place rhubarb in unbaked pie shell. Mix well remaining ingredients. Pour over rhubarb. Makes 1 (8-inch) pie.

Ruth Stoltzfus

VANILLA PIE

Bottom Part:

1 c. brown sugar
1 c. dark molasses
2 Tbsp. flour
2 c. water
2 tsp. vanilla

Crumbs:

1 c. flour
½ c. brown sugar
¼ c. shortening
½ tsp. soda
½ tsp. baking powder

Combine ingredients for bottom part and cook until thickened. Pour into unbaked pie shell and bake at 375° for 40 to 45 minutes. Makes 2 pies.

Naomi Grace Zook
Edna Zook
Anna King

VANILLA PIE

1 c. sugar
1 c. molasses
1 Tbsp. flour
1 egg
1 tsp. vanilla
1 pt. boiling water
2 ½ c. flour
1 c. sugar
½ c. lard
1 tsp. soda
1 tsp. cream of tartar

Boil the 1 cup sugar, molasses, 1 tablespoon flour and egg in boiling water. Cool and add vanilla. Mix and add the 2 ½ cups flour, 1 cup sugar, lard, soda and cream of tartar.

Barbie Zook
Liz Stoltzfus

RICE KRISPIE PIE

2 c. Rice Krispies
⅓ c. Karo
⅓ c. peanut butter

Mix together and press in pie shell. Fill with ice cream.

Rachel Esh

RICE KRISPIE PIE

4 eggs, beaten
1 c. molasses
1 c. granulated sugar
4 tsp. melted butter
2 tsp. vanilla
1 c. cold water
1 c. Rice Krispies
2 tsp. flour

Mix sugar and flour, then mix in the rest except beaten eggs. Stir eggs in last. Bake at 400° for about 35 to 40 minutes.

Priscilla King
Anna King

RICE CREAM PIE

½ c. corn syrup
½ c. peanut butter
3 c. Rice Krispies
1 qt. vanilla ice cream

Measure corn syrup and peanut butter into a large bowl. Stir until thoroughly combined. Add Rice Krispies. Mix until well coated. Press mixture evenly and firmly into a 9-inch pie pan. Chill until firm. Spread ice cream evenly in pie shell and serve or freeze to desire.

Mrs. Elam Z. Stoltzfus

WET BOTTOM SHOO-FLY PIES

3 c. molasses
1 c. brown sugar
3 c. boiling water
2 tsp. soda, dissolved in boiling water
8 eggs

Crumbs:

6 c. flour
2 c. brown sugar
1 tsp. soda
1 ½ c. shortening (lard)

Beat 4 cups crumbs with the molasses, brown sugar, boiling water, soda and eggs. Divide juice evenly into 5 or 6 (8-inch) pie crusts. Put rest of crumbs on top. Bake at 425° for 10 minutes, then at 350° for 45 minutes. Hardly ever runs over. Makes 5 or 6 pies.

Susie King

GOOEY SHOO-FLY PIE

Liquid:

6 eggs, beaten
1 c. granulated sugar
1 c. brown sugar
5 c. molasses (golden)
6 c. boiling water
2 heaping tsp. baking soda

Crumbs:

3 lb. regular flour
1 ½ lb. bread flour
2 ¾ lb. brown sugar
1 ¼ lb. lard
1 tsp. baking soda

Mix first 6 ingredients together and set aside. Mix crumb mixture all together until thoroughly mixed. Add 11 cups of crumbs to liquid mixture and mix well. Pour into 10 unbaked pie crusts. Baking time: 1 hour. Temperature: 350°.

Barbara King

SHOO-FLY PIE

1 c. King syrup
1 egg
¾ c. boiling water
1 tsp. soda
1 ¼ c. flour
⅔ c. brown sugar
2 Tbsp. margarine

Add the soda to the boiling water and put into refrigerator to cool. Set aside ½ cup crumbs to put on top. Mix the rest with juice. Bake at 375° for 10 minutes, then at 350° for 30 minutes.

Sylvia Petersheim

SHOO-FLY PIE

2 c. molasses
2 tsp. baking soda
⅓ c. brown sugar
2 ¼ c. boiling water

Mix together, then let cool.

Crumbs:

3 c. regular flour
2 c. whole wheat flour
1 tsp. soda
1 c. lard
2 c. brown sugar

Beat 2 eggs in molasses mixture, then add 3 ½ cups crumb mixture. Put into pie crusts, then sprinkle the rest of crumbs on top. Bake at 400° for 20 minutes, then at 375° for 25 minutes.

Mrs. Susie Smucker

SHOO-FLY PIE

2 c. molasses
4 eggs
1 c. brown sugar
2 c. boiling water
2 tsp. soda

Crumbs:

5 c. flour
2 c. brown sugar
1 c. lard

Mix well and add 3 heaping cupfuls crumbs to the gooey part and put the rest on top of pies. Makes 6 (8-inch) pies.

Naomi Petersheim

CHOCOLATE SHOO-FLY PIE

Pudding:

2 Tbsp. cornstarch
2 c. white sugar
2 Tbsp. flour
3 Tbsp. cocoa powder
2 eggs
2 c. water
1 tsp. vanilla
1 Tbsp. butter

Bring water to a boil. Add remaining ingredients and cook until it thickens. Cool and pour into 6 unbaked pie shells. Add topping. Bake and frost with chocolate frosting.

Top:

2 c. molasses
2 c. water (hot)
2 tsp. vanilla
2 c. brown sugar
1 c. shortening
2 eggs
½ c. cocoa powder
2 tsp. baking soda
¼ tsp. salt
½ tsp. cinnamon
5 c. flour

Mix molasses, water and vanilla. Set aside. Cream eggs, shortening and sugar. Add rest of ingredients, then add molasses mixture. Bake at 350° for 1 hour.

Katie King
(Hammertown)
Sylvia Petersheim

CUSTARD PIE

5 eggs, separated
1 c. sugar
1 tsp. cornstarch
½ can evaporated milk
1 qt. milk
1 tsp. vanilla

Beat egg yolks first, then add sugar, cornstarch and evaporated milk. Scald the milk. Beat egg whites and put in last. Bake at 350°.

Susie S. King

PEACH PIE

¼ c. granulated sugar
3 ½ Tbsp. flour
½ tsp. cinnamon
¼ tsp. salt
4 c. peaches, diced

Toss all together and put in unbaked pie shell.

Crumbs:

¼ c. butter
½ c. flour
¾ c. brown sugar

Mix and put on top. Bake at 425° for 35 to 40 minutes or until brown. Makes 1 (8-inch) pie.

Fannie Riehl

BLACK BOTTOM PIE

Filling:

2 sq. unsweetened chocolate
6 Tbsp. water
½ c. sugar
3 Tbsp. butter
¼ tsp. vanilla
pinch of salt

Crust:

1 ¼ c. chocolate wafers
¼ c. sugar
¼ c. melted butter

Reserve some crumbs for top of pie. Melt chocolate with water over low heat. Add sugar until dissolved and thickened, stirring constantly. Add butter and vanilla. Spread sauce over crust. Chill thoroughly. Fill with ice cream. Sprinkle crumbs on top. Bake at 375° for 5 to 8 minutes.

Rachel Esh

CHOCOLATE CHIFFON PIE

1 envelope unflavored gelatin
⅛ tsp. salt
¾ c. milk
1 c. icy cold evaporated milk, whipped
¾ c. sugar
1 egg yolk
3 sq. unsweetened chocolate
1 tsp. vanilla
whipped cream
1 (9-inch) baked pie shell

Mix gelatin, sugar and salt thoroughly in a saucepan. Beat egg yolk and milk together. Add to gelatin mixture. Add chocolate. Cook over medium heat, stirring constantly, until chocolate is melted. Do not boil. Remove from heat and beat with a beater until smooth. Place pan in bowl of ice water or chill in refrigerator, stirring occasionally until mixture mounds slightly when dropped from a spoon. Fold in whipped evaporated milk and vanilla. Turn into a baked pie shell and chill until firm. Top with whipped cream.

Linda Fisher

GRAPE-NUTS PIE

½ c. Grape-Nuts
½ c. water
1 c. brown sugar
1 c. King syrup
¼ c. butter
¼ tsp. salt
3 eggs, slightly beaten
¼ c. chopped pecans
1 tsp. vanilla

Mix Grape-Nuts with warm water. Let stand until water is soaked up. Meanwhile, combine sugar, syrup, butter, salt and eggs. Stir in softened cereal, nuts and vanilla. Pour in unbaked pie shell. Bake at 400° for 10 minutes, then at 350° for 25 minutes. Makes 1 (9-inch) pie.

Fannie Riehl

GERMAN CHEESE PIE

4 c. corn flakes, crushed to 1 c.
¼ c. packed brown sugar
5 Tbsp. butter or margarine, melted
1 (4 oz.) bar sweet cooking chocolate
1 (8 oz.) pkg. cream cheese, softened
½ c. packed brown sugar
1 tsp. vanilla
dash of salt
2 c. whipped topping

Preheat oven to 300°. Butter a 9-inch pie plate. Combine corn flake crumbs and brown sugar. Add butter. Mix thoroughly. Press evenly onto bottom and sides of pie plate. Bake 10 minutes. Cool. Heat water and chocolate in small saucepan over low heat until chocolate is just melted. Stir constantly. Let cool 10 to 15 minutes. In large bowl, mix cream cheese and sugar. Add vanilla and salt. Slowly beat chocolate into cheese mixture. Refrigerate 1 hour. Fold in whipped topping. Turn into crust. Freeze 4 hours. Makes 8 servings.

Sara Stoltzfoos

PEANUT BUTTER PIE

⅔ c. sugar
3 Tbsp. cornstarch
1 Tbsp. flour
pinch of salt
3 egg yolks
3 c. milk
2 Tbsp. butter
1 tsp. vanilla
¾ c. 10x sugar
½ c. peanut butter

Stir together the sugar, cornstarch, flour, pinch of salt, egg yolks, milk, butter and vanilla in saucepan over medium heat, stirring constantly. Mix the 10x sugar and peanut butter. Mix until crumbly. Sprinkle ⅔ cup peanut butter mixture into baked pie shell. Pour custard on top. Spread beaten egg whites to taste. Sprinkle remaining crumbs on top. Bake at 350° until brown.

Naomi Grace Zook

PEANUT BUTTER PIE

1 (8 oz.) cream cheese
1 c. 10x sugar
½ c. peanut butter
1 (8 oz.) Cool Whip

Mix cream cheese and 10x sugar well. Add peanut butter, then Cool Whip. Put in graham cracker crust.

Mary Stoltzfus
Rachel Esh

SNITZ PIE

1 gal. apple butter
6 qt. applesauce
14 c. sugar
1 tsp. salt
2 tsp. cinnamon
¾ tsp. nutmeg
2 c. clear jell or flour

Mix clear jell and sugar, then add enough water to make it runny. Add to rest of ingredients. Pour into unbaked pie shells and put a dough top on. Make a hole in center of dough. Brush top of pies with well beaten eggs, then sprinkle with crumbs. Bake at 350° for 1 hour. Makes 22 (8-inch) pies.

Crumbs:

1 c. flour
¼ c. lard
½ c. brown sugar

Mix until fine.

Mary Stoltzfus
Nancy Ann Esch

SNITZ

½ gal. snitz, cooked and put through strainer
1 ½ qt. applesauce
4 c. sugar
1 Tbsp. (rounded) cinnamon
1 tsp. nutmeg
1 Tbsp. lemon flavoring
add a little instant tapioca

Rachel Esh

CHURCH APPLE PIES

2 heaping c. apples, sliced roughly
water to cover apples
1 c. granulated sugar
¼ tsp. salt
1 c. water
2 Tbsp. clear jell

Mix sugar and salt with 1 cup water. Mix clear jell with water. When apples show a sign of boiling, put sugar in and slowly add clear jell to thicken. (Do not overcook.)

Katie S. King
Susie S. King

APPLE PIE FILLING

3 qt. apples, sliced
4 c. water
2 c. brown sugar
2 c. white sugar
4 Tbsp. butter
sprinkle of cinnamon

Cook apples until soft, then thicken with clear jell.

Elizabeth Stoltzfus

PIE CRUST

25 lb. flour
1 gal. lard
1 can Crisco
12 Tbsp. salt
12 Tbsp. baking powder
1 ½ lb. 10x sugar

This is large enough for church. Have lard stiff and cold before adding.

Susie King

PIE DOUGH

24 lb. pastry flour
1 ½ c. powdered sugar
1 c. baking powder
6 Tbsp. salt
12 lb. lard

Plenty for 60 pies.

Katie S. King
Scilla King

MINCEMEAT

a little more apples than meat
1 quart molasses
2 c. brown sugar to taste
2 c. granulated sugar to taste
1 Tbsp. allspice
2 Tbsp. cinnamon
2 c. vinegar
a little water

Cook slowly for 4 or 5 hours. Stir every now and then.

Katie S. King

MINCEMEAT

1 bucket apples
½ bucket ground meat
½ bucket cider
2 ½ lb. raisins
7 lb. sugar
1 ½ tsp. each cloves, cinnamon and allspice

Measure apples before grinding. Hard cider is best.

Rachel Esh

GRANDMOTHER'S PIE DOUGH

6 lb. flour
¼ c. sugar
¼ c. baking powder
3 lb. lard
1 ½ Tbsp. salt (if you wish)

Mix with 3 tablespoons water, vinegar or milk.

Priscilla King
Sara Stoltzfus

For A Larger Goe (Pie Dough):

24 lb. flour
1 ½ c. sugar
1 c. baking powder
12 lb. lard
6 Tbsp. salt

Sara Stoltzfus

PIE CRUST

3 c. flour
1 c. lard
2 Tbsp. granulated sugar

Mix with water.

Priscilla King

PIE CRUMBS

4 ½ lb. flour
2 lb. lard or Crisco
½ c. cornstarch
½ Tbsp. baking powder
1 c. 10x sugar
½ Tbsp. salt

Store unused crumbs in Tupperware and keep in a cool place.

Fannie Riehl

PIE DOUGH CRUST

9 lb. regular flour
3 ¼ lb. lard
1 c. cornstarch
2 Tbsp. baking powder
2 c. 10x sugar or brown sugar
2 Tbsp. salt

Mix all together and use as needed. To 10 cups crumbs put 2 tablespoons vinegar and add enough cold water to roll. Makes about 30 (9-inch) pies.

Susie Smucker
Linda Fisher

EASY PIE CRUST

3 c. flour
1 c. shortening
½ tsp. salt
½ c. water
1 egg, beaten with fork
1 Tbsp. vinegar

Mix flour, shortening and salt. In a separate bowl mix water, egg and vinegar, then pour into flour mixture. Form into a soft dough.

(Willie) Anna Fisher

LYDIA'S PIE DOUGH MIX

9 lb. flour
4 lb. lard
1 c. cornstarch
1 Tbsp. baking powder
2 c. brown sugar
1 Tbsp. salt

Mix all together. Wet with water or milk.

Linda Fisher

PIE DOUGH

4 c. flour
1 c. lard
1 tsp. salt
a little baking soda

Add water until moist.

Naomi Petersheim

SUNSHINE PIE

A pound of patience you must find;
Mixed well with loving words so kind.
Drop in 2 pounds of helpful deeds
And thoughts of other people's needs.
A peck of smiles will make the crust;
Then stir and bake it well, you must.
And now I'll ask that you may try a slice
Of my Sunshine Pie.

-• EXTRA RECIPES •-

Apple

An apple instead of a tranquilizer? A study at Michigan State University indicates that this works. The study, revealing fewer tensions, headaches, and emotional upsets, involved 2 apples a day.

Did you know that an apple a day can keep the dentist away? Apples play an important role in cleansing the teeth of decay-causing refined carbohydrates. The food removes debris, stimulates gum tissue, and also stimulates salivary flow.

Store apples away from onions and potatoes to prevent the absorption of their odors.

Apples can be a remedy for diarrhea: scrape the apple for babies, or simmer the parings in skim milk.

If your apples age before you can eat them, try drying them thoroughly and then carving them into faces. They can be attached to sticks and dressed. Apple dolls were a favorite toy in colonial America.

Cakes, Cookies & Desserts

"Cooks would never have created them so good to the taste, if they hadn't meant them to be eaten."

"Look first that your range heat be right,
And your hand be neat and skilled;
For the love of man oft takes its flight,
If his stomach be not filled."

Every minute you are angry,
you loose sixty seconds of happiness.

Double Pay

Some women say it doesn't pay
To bake in the old-fashioned way;
To fuss with recipes for cakes,
To beat, to measure, and to bake,
They say it's just a waste of time
When you can buy it for a dime!
Perhaps they're right, but here's the why
That I bake cookies, bead and pie:
If they could watch a boy's bright eyes,
And thrill at his unfeigned surprise,
If they could see that knowing look
That says, "Oh Mom, you sure can cook!"
They'd know that I get double pay
For all my time on baking day!

CAKES, COOKIES & DESSERTS

A LOVE CAKE FOR MOTHER

1 c. obedience
several lb. affections
1 pt. neatness
some holidays, birthday and everyday surprises
1 c. running errands
1 box powdered (willing) get up when I should
1 bottle "keep sunny all day long"
1 c. pure thoughtfulness

Mix well and bake in a hearty warm oven and serve to "Mother" everyday. She likes it in big slices!

CHOCOLATE FROSTING

2 pkg. melted chocolate
2 tsp. corn syrup
2 tsp. vanilla
3 Tbsp. soft butter
3 Tbsp. milk
3 ½ c. confectioners sugar

Mix chocolate, corn syrup, vanilla, butter and milk. Add confectioners sugar a little at a time. Beat until well blended.

Fannie Riehl

DELICIOUS ICING

2 pkg. Dream Whip
1 ½ c. Crisco
½ c. water
2 tsp. white vanilla
10 c. 4x sugar

Mix sugar in a little at a time. Mix real well.

Susie S. King

FLUFFY ICING

2 c. 10x sugar
4 Tbsp. flour
2 Tbsp. milk
1 ½ c. Crisco
2 tsp. vanilla

Mix thoroughly. Add 4 egg whites, beaten. Add 2 cups marshmallows, if you wish.

Susie S. King

MAGIC QUICK CHOCOLATE FROSTING

15 oz. can sweetened condensed milk
1 Tbsp. water
½ tsp. salt
½ tsp. vanilla
1 ½ sq. unsweetened chocolate

Put milk, water and salt in top of double boiler. Mix well. Add chocolate. Cook over rapidly boiling water, stirring often until thick, about 7 minutes. Remove from heat. Cool. Stir in vanilla. Spread on cake.

Fannie Riehl

CHOCOLATE ICING DELUXE

1 large egg
2 c. 10x sugar
¼ tsp. salt
⅓ c. butter
2 sq. unsweetened chocolate
1 tsp. vanilla

Beat egg with beater until fluffy. Sift sugar and add to egg. Add salt, shortening and melted chocolate. Beat until smooth and creamy. Add vanilla and spread on cake.

Sylvia Stoltzfus

FUDGE ICING

1 large egg
¼ tsp. salt
1 tsp. vanilla
2 c. 10x sugar
⅓ c. butter or margarine, soft
2 Tbsp. Crisco
5 Tbsp. cocoa

Melt the Crisco and cocoa and add to the rest. This is a soft icing and will not get hard.

Katie King
(Hammertown)

NO COOK MARSHMALLOW FROSTING

¼ tsp. salt
2 egg whites
¼ c. sugar
¾ c. Karo
¼ tsp. vanilla

Add salt to egg whites. Beat until soft peak. Gradually add sugar, one tablespoon at a time. Beat thoroughly after each addition.

Add Karo and vanilla, then beat until firmly peaked. Good on angel food and chiffon cakes.

Linda Fisher

CREAM CHEESE FROSTING

1 c. butter
1 (8 oz.) pkg. cream cheese
1 lb. 10x sugar
vanilla

Combine all ingredients and beat well. Frost cake when cool.

Naomi Grace Zook

BUTTER ICING

3 Tbsp. flour
1 c. milk
½ c. butter
½ c. Crisco
1 c. sugar
2 tsp. vanilla

Blend flour and milk. Cook together until thick. Let stand to cool. Cream butter and Crisco, then add sugar and vanilla. Add flour mixture. Beat 15 minutes or until icing is white.

Naomi Grace Zook

CHOCOLATE "PHILLY" FROSTING

1 (8 oz.) pkg. cream cheese
1 Tbsp. milk
1 tsp. vanilla
dash of salt
5 c. 10x sugar
3 (1 oz.) sq. unsweetened chocolate, melted

Combine softened cream cheese, milk, vanilla and salt, mixing until well blended. Add sugar, one cup at a time, mixing well after each addition. Stir in chocolate. Fills and frosts two 8 or 9-inch cake layers.

Sam Stoltzfoos

CREAM CHEESE FROSTING

½ c. margarine
1 (8 oz.) pkg. cream cheese, softened
1 tsp. vanilla
1 box 10x sugar

Cream together margarine, cream cheese and vanilla in bowl at medium speed. Gradually add 10x sugar, beating well until smooth. If mixture is too thick to spread, add a little milk.

(Vern) Mary Ann Paul

ANGEL FOOD CAKE

1 ¼ c. sifted cake flour
½ c. sugar
1 ½ c. egg whites
¼ tsp. salt
1 ¼ tsp. cream of tartar
1 tsp. vanilla
¼ tsp. almond extract
1 ⅓ c. sugar

Sift the cake flour and sugar together 4 times. Combine egg whites, vanilla, cream of tartar, salt and almond extract. Beat until soft peaks form. Sprinkle in sugar in 4 additions. Beat until blended. Sift in flour in 4 additions, folding in with large spoon. Turn bowl often. Do not beat. Pour into ungreased tube pan. Bake at 375° for 35 to 40 minutes. Cool cake upside down in pan. When cool, loosen sides and remove.

Helen Miller

BLACK JOE CAKE

2 c. brown sugar
2 c. flour
¾ c. cocoa
2 tsp. soda
1 tsp. baking powder
2 eggs
1 c. mix
½ c. hot coffee
½ c. vegetable oil

Bake at 350° for 30 minutes. May add topping.

Topping:

2 tsp. cocoa
1 c. sugar
1 c. hot water
1 Tbsp. cornstarch
1 Tbsp. butter
½ tsp. salt
1 tsp. vanilla

Mix cocoa, hot water, sugar and salt. Bring to a boil. Mix cornstarch with water. Stir. Add butter and vanilla

Barbie Zook
Sylvia Petersheim
Rachel King

CHOCOLATE CAKE

2 eggs, well beaten
2 c. granulated sugar
½ c. oil
½ c. cocoa
2 c. flour
1 c. milk
1 c. coffee, brewed
2 tsp. baking soda
2 tsp. baking powder

Bake at 350° for 30 minutes.

Liz Stoltzfus

MOIST CHOCOLATE CAKE

1 ½ c. sugar
1 c. oil
2 eggs
2 c. applesauce
2 c. flour
½ c. cocoa
¼ tsp. salt
2 tsp. soda

Cream the sugar and oil. Add the eggs and applesauce. Sift the flour, cocoa, salt and soda. Bake at 350° for 30 minutes.

Fudge Icing:

1 large egg
¼ tsp. salt
1 tsp. vanilla
2 c. 10x sugar
⅓ c. margarine
2 Tbsp. Crisco
5 Tbsp. cocoa

Melt Crisco and cocoa and add to the rest.

Ruth Stoltzfus

CHOCOLATE CAKE

2 c. brown sugar
½ c. lard
2 eggs
1 tsp. vanilla
1 c. milk
½ c. water
2 ½ c. flour
3 Tbsp. cocoa
1 tsp. soda
½ tsp. cream of tartar

Mix together brown sugar, lard, eggs and vanilla, then add milk. Sift flour, cocoa, soda and cream of tartar, then add water. Bake at 350° for 40 to 45 minutes.

Mrs. Edna B. Zook

CHOCOLATE CAKE

2 c. sugar
2 eggs
½ c. butter
1 ½ c. buttermilk
1 tsp. soda
1 tsp. baking powder
dash of salt
1 tsp. vanilla
½ c. cocoa
2 c. flour

Beat sugar, eggs and butter. Add vanilla. Mix soda with buttermilk. Mix dry ingredients. Alternate buttermilk with dry ingredients. Bake at 350° for 30 to 35 minutes.

Linda Fisher

EGGLESS CHOCOLATE CAKE

3 c. granulated sugar
1 c. lard
2 large Tbsp. cocoa
3 c. sour milk
3 tsp. soda
2 tsp. salt
vanilla
5 c. flour

Bake at 350°.

Sara Stoltzfus

ANGEL FOOD CAKE

1 ½ c. egg whites
1 ½ c. white sugar
1 ½ tsp. cream of tartar
1 c. cake flour
½ tsp. salt
1 tsp. almond flavoring

Sift together ¾ cup of the sugar and the flour three times. Set aside. Beat egg whites until frothy. Add salt and cream of tartar. Beat until it stands in peaks. Add ¾ cup of the sugar, about 3 tablespoons at a time, beating well with eggbeater each time, after adding the sugar. Lightly fold in the sugar-flour mixture, adding about ½ cup at a time. Add flavoring. Bake at 375° for about 35 to 40 minutes.

Anna King
Mrs. Edna B. Zook

JELLY ROLL (YELLOW)

¾ c. flour
¾ tsp. baking powder
¼ tsp. salt
4 eggs
¾ c. sugar
1 tsp. vanilla

Sift dry ingredients together. Beat egg whites until stiff. Add yellow of eggs and mix well. Gradually add sugar and beat until light colored. Add vanilla. Fold in flour. Line a 15 x 10-inch pan with wax paper. Spread batter evenly. Bake at 400° for 12 minutes. Turn cake onto a cloth sprinkled with 10x sugar. Remove paper and roll cake and cloth. Unroll again.

Elsie Kauffman

STRAWBERRY ANGEL CAKE DESSERT

- ½ angel food cake
- 1 box instant vanilla pudding
- 1 c. cold milk
- 1 pt. vanilla ice cream
- 1 box strawberry jello
- 1 c. boiling water
- 1 (10 oz.) frozen strawberries

Break cake in small pieces in an 8 x 12-inch dish. Dissolve pudding in milk. Add ice cream and beat until well mixed. Pour on cake. (Do not stir.) Let set. Dissolve jello in boiling water. Add strawberries. Stir until it begins to thicken. Pour over cake. Do not stir.

Mary Stoltzfus

CHOCOLATE JELLY ROLL

- 5 egg yolks, beaten
- 1 c. 10x sugar
- ¼ c. fine flour, sifted
- 5 stiffly beaten egg whites
- ½ tsp. salt
- 3 Tbsp. cocoa
- 1 tsp. vanilla

Add egg whites last and fold lightly to rest of ingredients. Bake at 350° for 10 to 12 minutes. Dump on lightly (10x) sugared cloth.

Filling:

- 1 c. milk
- 1 Tbsp. cornstarch
- ½ c. Crisco
- ¼ c. butter
- 1 c. 10x sugar

Boil the milk and cornstarch and stir until thickened. Cool. Cream the Crisco, butter and 10x sugar. Add cornstarch mixture to Crisco mixture one teaspoon at a time and beat until fluffy.

Naomi King

CRUMB CAKE

2 ½ c. flour
2 c. brown sugar
½ tsp. salt
½ c. shortening
1 c. sour milk
1 egg
¾ tsp. baking soda
1 tsp. vanilla

Mix flour, sugar, salt and shortening in small crumb-like form. Remove 1 cup crumbs. Add the rest of the ingredients to crumb mixture. Mix until smooth. Place the 1 cup crumbs on top. Bake 30 minutes or more at 350°.

Fannie Riehl
Mary Stoltzfus

OLD FASHION CRUMB CAKE

1 ½ c. brown sugar
2 to 3 c. flour
½ c. lard
1 egg
1 c. sour milk
1 tsp. baking soda
1 tsp. cinnamon
½ tsp. nutmeg
½ tsp. salt
1 tsp. vanilla

Mix the brown sugar, flour and lard until fine and crumbly. Reserve ½ cup. To the rest, add the remaining ingredients. Pour into floured cake pan and sprinkle remaining crumbs on top. Bake at 350° for 45 minutes.

Nancy Ann Esch

SOUR CREAM COFFEE CAKE

Topping:

⅓ c. brown sugar
¼ c. granulated sugar
2 tsp. cinnamon
½ c. chopped pecans

Cake:

½ c. butter, softened
1 c. sugar
2 eggs
1 c. sour cream
1 tsp. vanilla
2 c. flour
1 tsp. baking powder
1 tsp. baking soda
¼ tsp. salt

Combine all topping ingredients. Set aside.

For Cake: Cream butter and sugar in a bowl. Add eggs, sour cream and vanilla. Mix well. Combine dry ingredients. Add to butter and egg mixture. Pour half into greased 13 x 9-inch pan. Sprinkle with half the topping mixture. Add remaining half batter and topping mixture. Bake at 325° for 40 minutes.

Mary Ann Smucker

COFFEE CAKE

Batter:

3 c. flour
½ tsp. salt
6 tsp. baking powder
1 ½ c. sugar
½ c. shortening
2 eggs
1 c. milk

Topping:

1 c. brown sugar
4 tsp. cinnamon
4 Tbsp. flour
4 Tbsp. melted butter
1 c. nuts

Cream sugar and shortening. Add eggs and milk. Sift together flour, baking powder and salt for topping. Melt butter and mix to crumb consistency. Put half of batter into a 9 x 13-inch greased cake pan. Top with half of topping. Repeat. Bake at 350° for 30 to 35 minutes.

Rachel Esh

STREUSEL COFFEE CAKE

1 egg
½ c. milk
¾ c. sugar
½ c. Crisco oil
2 tsp. baking powder
½ tsp. salt
1 ½ c. sifted flour

Combine sugar, Crisco oil and egg. Add milk. Beat thoroughly. Stir in combined dry ingredients. Beat until smooth. Put in pan. Sprinkle with streusel topping. Bake at 375° for 30 to 35 minutes.

Topping:

½ c. brown sugar
2 Tbsp. flour
2 tsp. cinnamon
2 Tbsp. Crisco oil
½ c. firmly chopped nuts

Priscilla Fisher

COFFEE CAKE

1 box instant pudding (vanilla)
1 box instant pudding (butterscotch)
1 c. oil
1 c. water
1 cake mix (white or yellow)
4 eggs

Mix together.

Topping:

1 tsp. cinnamon
1 c. brown sugar and nuts

Between batter and on top.

Rachel King

COFFEE CAKE

1 box white or yellow cake mix
1 box instant vanilla pudding
1 box instant butterscotch pudding
4 eggs
1 c. vegetable oil
1 c. water

Mix all ingredients together.

Topping or Crumbs:

1 c. brown sugar
1 c. ground nuts
2 tsp. cinnamon

Mix together. Put half of cake dough in a 9 x 13-inch cake pan. Sprinkle half of topping on cake, then put rest of dough on and the remaining crumbs on top of cake. Bake at 350° for 40 minutes or until done.

Katie King
(Hammertown)

FRUIT CAKE

1 ¼ c. sugar
2 eggs
½ c. vegetable oil
1 c. applesauce
2 c. flour
2 tsp. baking soda
½ tsp. salt
1 ½ c. peaches, drained (any other fruit may be used)

Combine all ingredients and mix well. Bake at 350° for 30 minutes.

Frosting:

½ c. butter
1 pkg. cream cheese
2 or 3 c. 10x sugar
vanilla

Soften butter and cream cheese and mix well with 10x sugar. Frost cake when cool.

Elizabeth Stoltzfus
Barbie Zook

APPLESAUCE OR FRUIT CAKE

2 c. all-purpose flour
1 c. whole wheat flour
2 c. brown sugar
3 eggs
2 c. thick applesauce
1 c. buttermilk
2 tsp. soda
½ tsp. salt
1 tsp. cinnamon (if desired)
½ c. vegetable oil

Mix all together and bake at 350° for 40 to 45 minutes. When cake is warm from oven, put topping on and brown under broiler.

Topping:

⅔ c. brown sugar
1 c. coconut
1 c. chopped nuts (if desired)
6 tsp. melted butter
¼ c. cream
1 tsp. vanilla

Elsie Kauffman

FRUIT COCKTAIL CAKE

2 c. flour
1 ½ c. granulated sugar
2 c. fruit cocktail (level)
2 tsp. soda
2 eggs, beat 2 minutes

Bake 40 minutes at 350°.

Icing:

¾ c. granulated sugar
½ c. canned milk
¾ stick margarine

Cook 7 minutes, stirring all the time. Sprinkle with nuts.

Katie S. King

APPLE CAKE

3 eggs
1 ½ c. oil
2 c. sugar
3 c. flour
1 tsp. baking soda
1 tsp. vanilla
½ tsp. salt
½ tsp. nutmeg
½ tsp. cinnamon
4 c. apples
1 c. chopped nuts

Mix the eggs, oil and sugar. Mix the flour, baking soda, vanilla, salt, nutmeg, cinnamon, apples and nuts. Bake at 350°.

Topping:

½ stick butter
1 c. brown sugar
¼ c. milk
1 tsp. vanilla

Bring to a boil together. Boil 4 minutes. Spoon over warm cake.

Naomi King
Liz Stoltzfus

GERMAN APPLE CAKE

½ c. Crisco
½ c. granulated sugar
½ c. brown sugar
3 eggs
2 ¼ c. flour
¼ tsp. salt
2 tsp. soda
1 c. sour milk
1 tsp. cinnamon
2 c. raw apples

Beat sugar, shortening and eggs until fluffy. Add milk and dry ingredients. Fold in apples. Pour in greased pan and bake at 350° for 45 minutes.

Topping:

½ c. brown sugar
¼ c. granulated sugar
½ tsp. cinnamon
½ c. chopped nuts

Put this on top of cake before baking.

Susie S. King

APPLE WALNUT CAKE

3 eggs, beaten
2 c. sugar
½ c. vegetable oil
2 tsp. vanilla
2 c. flour
2 tsp. baking soda
2 tsp. cinnamon
½ tsp. nutmeg
¼ tsp. salt
4 c. diced, unpeeled apples
1 c. coarsely chopped walnuts

Cream Cheese Frosting:

2 (3 oz.) cream cheese
¼ c. butter or margarine
1 ½ c. confectioners sugar
½ tsp. vanilla

Bake at 325° for 50 to 60 minutes.

Barbie Zook

BUTTERSCOTCH APPLE CAKE

1 c. vegetable oil
2 c. sugar
2 eggs
2 ½ c. flour (Pillsbury or Gold Medal)
1 tsp. cinnamon
1 tsp. baking soda
1 tsp. baking powder
1 tsp. salt
3 c. chopped apples
1 c. butterscotch chips

Mix oil, sugar and eggs together and blend in flour, cinnamon, soda, baking powder and salt. Stir in the chopped apples. Spread in a 13 x 9-inch pan. Sprinkle butterscotch chips on top. Bake at 325° for 15 minutes, then reduce heat to 300° for 55 minutes. Serve plain or with ice cream. Very good.

Susie Smucker

PUMPKIN ROLL

Cake:

3 eggs)
1 c. sugar
⅔ c. pumpkin
2 tsp. cinnamon
1 tsp. lemon juice
¾ c. flour
1 tsp. baking powder
½ tsp. salt

Filling:

1 c. 10x sugar
4 Tbsp. butter
1 (8 oz.) cream cheese, soft
½ tsp. vanilla

Beat eggs at high speed for 5 minutes. Mix in the rest of ingredients. Grease and flour jelly roll pan before pouring batter on. Bake at 375° for 15 minutes only. Cool 5 minutes and turn upside down on towel sprinkled with 10x sugar. Store in refrigerator after putting filling on roll. (Use a linen tea towel so you don't get a lot of fuzz on cake.)

Katie King
Rachel Esh
(Hammertown)

PUMPKIN CAKE

1 ½ c. sugar
½ c. Crisco
2 eggs
½ tsp. salt
1 tsp. cinnamon
1 tsp. ginger
1 tsp. nutmeg
1 c. pumpkin
¾ c. milk
3 tsp. baking powder
½ tsp. baking soda
½ c. nuts
2 c. flour

Mix all together well. Place in a 13 x 9-inch pan. Bake at 375° about 1 hour.

(Vern) Mary Ann Paul

POKE CAKE

Use any good white cake recipe or cake mix and bake according to directions, then cool. Poke with a fork at ½-inch intervals. Dissolve 1 box gelatin in hot water. Add cold water according to directions and pour over cake. Chill 3 to 4 hours. Top with Cool Whip.

Rachel Esh

JAM CAKE

1 c. sugar
½ c. margarine
1 egg
1 c. sour milk
2 ½ c. flour
1 tsp. baking soda and cinnamon
½ tsp. cloves
1 c. jam (any kind)

Mix together well. Bake at 350° until done. When cold put a drop of jam on top. No icing is needed.

(Vern) Mary Ann Paul

BOSTON CREME CAKE

4 egg yolks
¾ c. water
1 ½ c. sugar
2 c. flour
3 tsp. baking powder
4 egg whites
½ tsp. salt

Filling:

3 c. milk
1 heaping Tbsp. flour
1 heaping Tbsp. cornstarch
1 c. sugar
2 eggs

Beat 4 egg yolks and water until stiff. Gradually add sugar and beat again. Sift flour and baking powder and add to mixture. Fold in stiffly beaten egg whites (salt added to egg whites). Bake at 350°.

Filling: Heat milk and sugar to almost boiling point. Mix flour, cornstarch and eggs and add a little milk to make a paste. Stir this into your milk. Slice cake through middle. Put filling in. Save some filling for top and add cocoa.

Mary Stoltzfus

BOSTON CREAM PIE

4 egg yolks
9 Tbsp. water
1 ½ c. sugar
2 c. flour
3 tsp. baking powder
½ tsp. salt

Chocolate Glaze:

2 Tbsp. butter
1 sq. unsweetened chocolate or 1 Tbsp. cocoa
1 c. 10x sugar
2 Tbsp. boiling water

Beat egg yolks. Add water, beating well. Add sugar slowly, beating all the while. Sift the flour. Put in baking powder and salt. Add to first mixture. Beat real good. Beat egg whites until stiff and fold into batter. Pour in cake pan. Bake at 350° for 30 to 35 minutes.

Creme Filling:

½ c. sugar
¼ c. cornstarch
¼ tsp. salt
2 c. milk
4 egg yolks
½ tsp. vanilla

Heat milk. Mix sugar, egg yolks, cornstarch and salt. Slowly add to milk and stir until thick.

Priscilla Fisher
Susie S. King
Sylvia Petersheim

BOSTON CREME PIE

2 c. bread flour
1 tsp. baking powder
½ tsp. salt
½ c. oil
3 eggs
1 tsp. vanilla
1 c. milk
2 c. sugar
2 tsp. soda
2 tsp. vinegar

Sift together the bread flour, baking powder and salt. Add the oil, eggs, vanilla, milk and sugar. Mix well. Mix the soda and vinegar. Add to cake mixture. Bake for 30 minutes at 350°. This makes 2 (8-inch) round cakes, but only one cut in half, is needed.

Custard Filling:

1 c. milk, scalded
⅓ c. sugar
pinch of salt
2 heaping Tbsp. cornstarch
2 eggs
1 Tbsp. butter
vanilla

Scald milk. Mix together the sugar, pinch of salt and cornstarch. Add hot milk to sugar mixture. Cook together until thick. Beat the eggs and add the hot mixture to eggs and boil over low heat for 3 minutes and add butter and vanilla.

Chocolate Glaze:

2 Tbsp. butter
¼ c. chocolate chips
¼ c. 10x sugar
2 Tbsp. hot water

Melt together the butter and chocolate chips. Cool, then add the 10x sugar and hot water.

Elizabeth Stoltzfus

DATE CAKE

2 c. sugar (white)
2 eggs
2 Tbsp. butter
2 c. ground dates, mixed with 2 c. boiling water
3 c. flour
2 tsp. soda
2 c. walnuts

Bake at 375° for 45 minutes.

Rachel Esh

SOUR CREAM SPICE CAKE

½ c. shortening
2 c. brown sugar
3 egg yolks, beaten
1 c. sour cream
1 tsp. soda
1 tsp. vanilla
2 tsp. cinnamon
1 tsp. cloves
1 tsp. allspice
1 ¾ c. flour
½ tsp. salt

Fold in stiffly beaten egg whites last. Bake at 350° for 30 minutes.

Fannie Riehl

PEANUT BUTTER TASTY CAKE

4 eggs
2 c. flour
2 c. sugar
2 tsp. baking powder
2 Tbsp. butter
dash of salt
1 c. milk
½ c. margarine
1 tsp. vanilla

Grease and flour a cookie sheet with sides. Mix all ingredients. Bake at 350° for 20 to 25 minutes. Remove from oven and spread with 1 cup peanut butter. Cool. Melt 1 large bag of milk chocolate chips in double boiler. Spread over cooled peanut butter. Do not refrigerate.

Fannie Riehl

EVERYBODY'S CAKE

3 eggs
1 ½ c. sugar
½ c. vegetable oil
1 c. milk
1 tsp. vanilla
2 tsp. baking powder
2 ½ c. flour

Mix all ingredients together. Bake at 350° for 30 to 35 minutes.

Linda Fisher

HAWAIIAN WEDDING CAKE

1 yellow cake mix
1 (20 oz.) can pineapple (crushed)
1 (8 oz.) pkg. cream cheese
2 c. milk
1 (3 oz.) pkg. instant vanilla pudding
whipped cream

Bake cake according to directions on package. Punch holes in top of cake to allow pineapple and juice to penetrate. Cool. Spoon pineapple and juice on top of cake. Beat together cream cheese, pudding mix and milk. After mixture thickens, spread over pineapple. Top with whipped cream to serve. Store in refrigerator.

Barbara King

STRAWBERRY OR PEACH SHORTCAKE

2 c. peaches
sugar
½ c. jello
2 ¼ c. flour
1 ½ c. sugar
½ c. shortening
1 c. milk
3 tsp. baking powder
½ tsp. salt
1 tsp. vanilla
3 eggs

Mix the peaches with sugar and jello. Let stand until dough is mixed. Bake at 350° for 45 to 50 minutes or until golden brown. Spoon peach mixture over dough.

Fannie Glick

STRAWBERRY SHORTCAKE

2 ½ c. flour
2 tsp. baking powder
½ tsp. salt
2 eggs
1 c. sugar
1 c. milk
2 Tbsp. butter
1 tsp. vanilla

Sift flour, baking powder and salt. Beat eggs and add sugar, milk and flavoring. Combine egg mixture with dry ingredients. Add melted butter and beat well. Pour into 2 greased 8-inch cake pans. Spread strawberry whip between layers and on top.

To Make Whip:

1 c. sugar
½ c. water
2 stiffly beaten egg whites
2 c. crushed strawberries

Boil the sugar and water together until clear. Pour syrup over egg whites. Add strawberries.

Sylvia Petersheim
Mary Stoltzfus

OATMEAL CAKE

1 ⅞ c. boiling water
1 ½ c. quick oatmeal
¾ c. shortening
1 ½ c. brown sugar
1 ½ c. white sugar
3 eggs
2 ¼ c. flour
1 ½ tsp. nutmeg
1 ½ tsp. cinnamon
¾ tsp. salt
1 ½ tsp. vanilla

Topping:

1 c. brown sugar
1 ½ c. nuts
1 ½ c. coconut
9 Tbsp. melted butter
⅓ c. cream
1 tsp. vanilla

Pour boiling water over oatmeal and let set 20 minutes. Cream shortening and sugar well. Add unbeaten eggs, one at a time, beating well after each one. Blend in oatmeal mixture. Sift flour, spices, soda and salt together and fold in. Bake in greased and floured pan at 350° for 30 to 35 minutes. While cake is still hot, pour on topping and put under broiler for 2 minutes or until brown.

Rachel Esh

FRESH PEACH UPSIDE-DOWN CAKE

Topping:

⅓ c. butter, melted
½ c. brown sugar

Cake Batter:

1 ⅓ c. Pillsbury flour
2 tsp. baking powder
1 egg
1 c. sugar
⅓ c. shortening
½ tsp. salt
⅔ c. milk
½ tsp. lemon juice
1 tsp. vanilla

Arrange peach slices in topping. Mix all ingredients together, except egg. Mix well. Add egg and mix well again. Pour over peach slices. Put into a 9 x 9-inch cake pan. Bake at 350° for 40 minutes. Let cool 5 to 10 minutes, then remove from pan.

Susie Smucker

CHOCOLATE CHIFFON CAKE

1 ½ c. sugar
1 ¾ c. flour
1 ½ tsp. soda
8 eggs, separated
2 tsp. vanilla
1 tsp. salt
½ c. vegetable oil
¼ c. cocoa
¾ c. boiling water
½ tsp. cream of tartar

First mix cocoa in boiling water. Let cool. Take sugar and flour (mix well). Put egg yolks, vanilla, salt and oil in. Stir in cocoa-water mixture. Put cream of tartar in egg whites and beat stiff. Put first mixture in. Beat egg whites. Bake in tube pan at 325° for 60 to 65 minutes.

Katie S. King

CARROT CAKE

2 c. sugar
2 c. flour
1 ½ c. vegetable oil
4 eggs
2 tsp. baking powder
1 ½ tsp. baking soda
2 tsp. cinnamon
2 ½ c. carrots, grated
1 tsp. salt

Frosting:

1 c. butter
1 (8 oz.) pkg. cream cheese
1 lb. confectioners sugar
vanilla

Mix all ingredients together. Pour into a 9 x 13-inch baking pan. Baking time: 50 minutes. Temperature: 350°.

Frosting: Combine all ingredients and beat well. Frost when cool.

Mrs. Elam Z. Stoltzfus
Barbara King
Liz Stoltzfus

BANANA CAKE

2 ½ c. flour
1 ¼ tsp. baking powder
1 ¼ tsp. soda
3 eggs
⅔ c. buttermilk
1 ¼ c. bananas
⅔ c. shortening
1 ⅓ c. sugar
1 ¼ tsp. salt

Cream shortening and sugar. Add eggs, sour milk and bananas. Add flour, baking powder, soda and salt. Bake in a 13 x 9 x 2-inch cake pan. Bake at 350° for 45 to 50 minutes.

Cream Cheese Frosting:

1 (8 oz.) pkg. cream cheese
1 box 10x sugar
½ stick butter
1 tsp. vanilla

Naomi Grace Zook
Ruth Stoltzfus

COWBOY CAKE

1 c. shortening
2 c. brown sugar
1 egg
1 c. thick milk (may use milk with 1 Tbsp. vinegar)
1 tsp. cinnamon
1 tsp. soda
2 ½ c. flour

Mix shortening, sugar and eggs, the add milk and flour.

Crumbs:

⅓ c. brown sugar
½ c. flour
1 Tbsp. butter

Place on top of cake before baking.

Liz Stoltzfus

PUDDING CAKE WITH JELLO

2 (3 oz.) boxes strawberry jello
1 ¾ c. boiling water
1 box cake mix, baked like directions on box

Pour hot jello mixture over warm cake that has been punched with a fork. Prepare 2 boxes instant pudding, like directions on box and spread on cake. Top with Cool Whip.

Liz Stoltzfus

FUNNEL CAKE

⅔ c. milk
1 egg
¼ tsp. salt (scant)
1 ¼ c. flour
2 Tbsp. sugar
1 tsp. baking powder

Beat egg with milk, then blend in flour, sugar, baking powder and salt. Drop batter into deep fat heated to 375°. Fry until puffy and golden brown, turning once. Remove and drain.

Liz Stoltzfus

CHOCOLATE CRAZY CAKE

¾ c. oil
2 Tbsp. vinegar
1 tsp. salt
2 c. sugar
2 c. cold water
2 tsp. vanilla
2 tsp. soda
⅓ c. cocoa
3 c. flour

Mix in given order. Bake at 350° for 35 to 40 minutes.

Naomi Grace Zook

CHOCOLATE JELLY ROLL

5 egg yolks, beaten
1 c. 10x sugar
¼ c. sifted cake flour
½ tsp. salt
3 Tbsp. cocoa (scant)
1 tsp. vanilla
5 stiffly beaten egg whites

Beat yolks. Add other ingredients, then blend in beaten whites. Bake on cookie sheet 10 to 15 minutes. Do not overbake. Place baked cake on a cloth sprinkled with 10x sugar. Roll up. When cool unroll and spread on filling. Reroll.

Filling for Jelly Roll:

1 c. milk
1 Tbsp. cornstarch
½ c. Crisco
¼ c. butter
1 c. 10x sugar

Boil the milk with the cornstarch. Cool. Cream the Crisco, butter and 10x sugar together. Add cooled milk to this one tablespoon at a time. Beat until fluffy.

Ruth Stoltzfus

MARSHMALLOW CAKES

½ c. butter
¾ c. sugar
2 eggs
1 tsp. vanilla
¾ c. flour
¼ tsp. baking powder
¼ tsp. salt
2 ½ c. miniature marshmallows
1 c. chocolate chips
1 c. peanut butter
1 ½ c. Rice Krispies

Bake the butter, sugar, eggs, vanilla, flour, baking powder and salt for 15 to 20 minutes at 350°. Add the marshmallows and bake 2 minutes longer. Cool 3 minutes. Melt the chocolate chips and mix peanut butter and Rice Krispies.

Anna King

PUMPKIN CAKE ROLL

3 eggs, beaten
1 c. sugar
¾ c. flour
⅔ c. pumpkin, cooked and mashed
1 tsp. baking soda
2 tsp. cinnamon

Beat eggs and add remaining ingredients. Beat together and spread on greased cookie sheet with sides and bake at 375° for 10 to 12 minutes. Loosen with a knife and turn over onto towel with 10x sugar spread over it. Roll with towel. Let cool. Unroll and put filling. Reroll and freeze, if desired.

Filling:

1 c. 10x sugar
8 oz. cream cheese
4 Tbsp. margarine
½ tsp. vanilla

Mix well.

(Vern) Mary Ann Paul

LAZY WOMAN'S CAKE

2 c. white sugar
5 Tbsp. carob or cocoa
2 tsp. soda
2 tsp. vinegar
2 c. cold water
3 c. flour
1 tsp. salt
¾ c. oil
1 tsp. vanilla

Put all ingredients in bowl, except 1 cup water. Mix well, then stir in last cup of water. Bake in pan 45 to 60 minutes at 350°. A very moist cake. May be used for cupcakes. Yields 30.

Mrs. Elam Z. Stoltzfus

WHITE TEXAS SHEET CAKE

1 c. water
1 c. butter or margarine
2 c. plus 2 Tbsp. sugar
2 c. plus 2 Tbsp. flour
½ tsp. salt
2 eggs
½ c. sour cream
1 tsp. baking soda
½ tsp. lemon extract
½ tsp. vanilla extract
rind of 1 lemon, grated

Boil together water and butter. Remove from heat and while hot, add flour, sugar and baking soda. Add lemon rind and extracts.

121722

Pour into greased and floured 11 x 14-inch jelly roll pan. Bake at 350° about 20 minutes.

Frosting:

½ c. butter or margarine
6 Tbsp. milk
3 ½ c. 10x sugar
½ tsp. lemon extract
½ tsp. vanilla extract
rind of 1 lemon, grated

Boil butter and milk. Remove from heat and stir in 10x sugar, lemon and extracts. Frost cake while warm. Cool and cut in bars.

Priscilla King

WATERGATE CAKE

1 pkg. white cake mix
3 eggs
1 c. club soda
1 c. oil
1 pkg. pistachio pudding
1 c. nuts

Icing:

1 (3 oz.) cream cheese
1 tsp. vanilla
¼ c. margarine
3 c. 10x sugar

Combine cake ingredients together and mix well. Bake in 13 x 9-inch pan at 350° for 45 minutes to 1 hour or until done.

(Vern) Mary Ann Paul

WATERGATE CAKE

1 box white cake mix
2 boxes pistachio pudding (instant)
½ c. oil
½ c. water
½ c. milk
5 eggs

Mix all ingredients together. Bake at 350° for 30 minutes.

Icing:

1 large container whipped topping
1 box instant pistachio pudding
½ pt. Dream Whip

Mix together whipped topping with instant pudding. Mix and add Dream Whip. Beat well and ice cake when cool.

Mary Ann Paul
Anna King

SHOO-FLY CAKE

1 pt. molasses
1 pt. hot boiling water
2 tsp. soda
2 eggs

Crumbs:

5 c. flour
2 c. brown sugar
½ c. lard

Put a little over half of the crumbs into the juice. Leave the rest for on top.

Anna King

CHOCOLATE BAR CAKE

6 egg yolks
1 c. sugar
⅔ c. water
1 ⅓ c. all-purpose flour
2 tsp. vanilla
⅓ c. cocoa
1 tsp. baking soda
½ tsp. salt
6 egg whites
1 c. sugar

In small bowl beat egg yolks about 3 minutes on high speed. Gradually add 1 cup sugar. Blend in water and vanilla on low speed. Combine flour, cocoa, baking soda and salt in small bowl. Add flour mixture beating until batter is smooth. Beat egg whites until foamy. Add sugar. Beat until stiff peaks form. Fold in chocolate mixture. Pour on paper lined cookie sheet . Bake at 375° for 18 to 20 minutes.

Priscilla King
Anna King
Susie King

HOT MILK SPONGE CAKE

4 eggs, well beaten
2 c. granulated sugar
2 c. flour
2 tsp. baking powder
1 c. milk
1 stick butter

Heat milk and butter until butter is melted. Set aside. Combine eggs and sugar. Add dry ingredients. Beat 1 minute. Add milk and butter mixture. Bake at 400° for 10 minutes, then at 350° for 20 minutes until done.

Mary Ann Smucker

MISSISSIPPI MUD CAKE

2 sticks butter, melted
½ c. cocoa
4 eggs, slightly beaten
2 c. sugar
1 ½ c. flour
1 ½ c. pecans, chopped

Mix together butter and cocoa. Add eggs and sugar. Blend flour, pecans, vanilla and salt into mixture. Bake 35 minutes at 350° in a greased 9 x 13-inch pan.

Topping:

mini marshmallows
1 box 10x sugar
½ c. milk
⅓ c. cocoa
1 stick butter

Cover cake with mini marshmallows and place in oven to melt some. Combine 10x sugar, milk, cocoa and melted butter. Mix until smooth. Spread over cake.

May Gay
Brooks, OR

ZUCCHINI CAKE

2 c. flour
2 c. sugar
1 Tbsp. cinnamon
1 tsp. salt
2 tsp. soda
1 tsp. baking powder
1 c. oil
3 eggs
2 tsp. vanilla
2 c. grated zucchini
1 ½ c. chopped nuts

In large bowl combine flour, cinnamon, baking soda, baking powder, salt, oil, vanilla and eggs. Beat at medium speed until well mixed. Stir in zucchini, raisins and 1 cup nuts. Pour into greased and floured 13 x 9 x 2-inch pan. Sprinkle with ½ cup nuts. Bake at 350° for 50 minutes.

Cream Cheese Frosting:

1 (8 oz.) pkg. cream cheese, softened
1 stick margarine or butter, softened
2 c. 10x sugar
1 tsp. vanilla
¼ c. cocoa (if desired)

Cream margarine and cream cheese well. Add vanilla. Beat in sugar a little at a time.

Priscilla King
Fannie Glick

CHOCOLATE ZUCCHINI CAKE

2 c. sugar
1 c. vegetable oil
3 eggs
2 ½ c. all-purpose flour
¼ c. cocoa
1 tsp. soda
1 tsp. baking powder
¼ tsp. salt
½ c. milk
2 c. zucchini
1 tsp. vanilla

Priscilla King

CREAMED FILLED CUPCAKES

3 c. flour
¾ c. cocoa
2 tsp. baking powder
2 tsp. soda
1 c. Wesson oil
2 ½ c. brown sugar
4 egg yolks
2 tsp. vanilla
1 tsp. salt
2 ¼ c. hot coffee

Combine the flour, cocoa, baking powder and soda. Mix oil, brown sugar, yolks, vanilla, salt and coffee. Beat egg whites and add last. Bake at 350°.

Filling:

3 c. milk
3 Tbsp. cornstarch
1 ¼ c. Crisco
1 ¼ c. margarine
3 c. 10x sugar

Heat the milk and cornstarch and set aside to cool. Cream the Crisco, margarine and 10x sugar.

Priscilla King

CHOCOLATE CREAM FILLED CUPCAKES

2 tsp. vanilla
1 c. salad oil
2 ½ c. sugar
1 tsp. salt
4 egg yolks
3 c. flour
1 c. cocoa
2 tsp. baking soda
2 tsp. baking powder
2 ¼ c. hot coffee
4 stiffly beaten egg whites

Mix the vanilla, oil, sugar, salt and egg yolks together. Sift the flour, cocoa, baking soda and baking powder. Add the hot coffee and add egg whites last. Bake at 350°.

Filling:

1 c. milk
1 Tbsp. cornstarch
½ c. Crisco
¼ c. butter
1 c. granulated sugar

Boil the milk and cornstarch. Cool. Mix the Crisco, butter and sugar. Mix together well. Add one tablespoon cornstarch mixture at a time. Stir until fluffy.

Barbara King

PARTY CUPCAKES

Use any good white cake recipe. Divide into portions and add a different flavor of undissolved jello to each portion. Put into cupcake pans and bake.

Rachel Esh

THRIFTY CUPCAKES

⅓ c. soft shortening
⅔ c. sugar
½ c. milk
1 tsp. vanilla
¼ tsp. walnut extract
1 ¼ c. flour
½ tsp. salt
1 ¾ tsp. baking powder
1 egg, beaten

Cream the shortening and sugar. Add the milk, vanilla and walnut extract. Sift together the flour, salt and baking powder and add to creamed mixture. Add the egg. Bake at 375° for 15 minutes. Makes 1 dozen. Frost with buttercream frosting. Put walnuts on top.

Rebecca K. Stoltzfus

KEUFELS

Dough:

1 c. plus 2 Tbsp. flour
½ c. butter or margarine
1 (3 oz.) cream cheese

Mix ingredients with a fork. Form into 24 small size balls and with finger press and shape into small size muffin tins.

Mix the following:

1 c. brown sugar
2 Tbsp. melted butter
1 tsp. vanilla
1 egg
¼ tsp. salt
¾ c. chopped nuts

Fill muffin tins. Bake 20 minutes at 350°.

Mary Stoltzfus

PUMPKIN CUPCAKES

2 c. pumpkin
2 c. sugar
4 eggs
¾ c. oil
2 c. flour
1 tsp. salt
1 tsp. baking powder
2 tsp. baking soda
1 tsp. cinnamon

Mix together pumpkin, sugar, eggs and oil. Sift flour, salt, baking powder, soda and cinnamon. Add to pumpkin mixture. Mix well, then put in cupcake pans. Bake at 350° for 20 to 30 minutes.

Mrs. Susie Smucker

CHERRY CHEESE CUPCAKES

3 pkg. cream cheese
⅔ c. sugar
3 eggs
1 Tbsp. vanilla
vanilla wafers
1 can pie filling

Mix all ingredients except wafers and pie filling. Place a wafer in the bottom of each cupcake paper. Fill ¾ full with cheese mixture. Bake at 350° for 15 minutes. Cool and top with pie filling.

Naomi Grace Zook

YUMMY CUPCAKES

2 c. granulated sugar
3 c. flour
½ c. cocoa
2 tsp. vanilla
12 oz. chocolate chips
2 tsp. baking soda
2 Tbsp. vinegar
⅔ c. vegetable oil
2 c. water

Filling:

8 oz. cream cheese
1 egg
⅓ c. sugar
dash of salt

Mix ingredients for dark part of cupcakes. Fill muffin tins lined with cupcake papers ½ full. Drop 1 teaspoon of white part in center of each cupcake. Bake at 350° until done.

Mary Stoltzfus

POEM

You can live without music
You can live without books
But show me the one who
Can live without cooks.

Susie King

SANDWICH COOKIES

4 ¾ c. light brown sugar
1 ½ c. butter and lard
1 ½ c. milk
1 egg
vanilla
1 Tbsp. cream of tartar
1 tsp. baking soda
12 or more c. flour

Cream sugar and shortening. Add egg, milk, vanilla, cream of tartar and soda can be added with flour. Roll. Cut into cookies and bake at 350°.

Mrs. Elam Z. Stoltzfus

PECAN SANDIES

1 c. butter (2 sticks)
1 c. sugar
2 egg yolks
1 tsp. vanilla
2 c. sifted flour
¼ tsp. salt
2 egg whites, beaten
1 ½ c. chopped pecans

Icing:

2 c. 10x sugar
2 Tbsp. butter
1 tsp. vanilla
2 to 3 Tbsp. hot water
green food coloring

Cream butter and sugar until fluffy. Add egg yolks and vanilla. Sift and add flour and salt. Chill dough for ease in handling. Shape into balls and dip in egg whites and roll in nuts. With finger, make a deep impression in center of each. Bake 15 minutes at 350°. Fill hole with icing.

Rachel Esh

THE INGREDIENTS

The sugar we use
    The taste to please
Shortening is needed
    The toughness to ease
The flour we add
    To make it firm
Also the eggs
    Under the same term.

Milk is required, for some that we make
    While this all depends on the quality of cake
A dash of salt,
    The taste to improve
Flavoring as desired
    Then may be used.

The leavening is added
    To make it light
But recipes are required
    To do it right
You prefer a nice cake,
    Then you may trust
That accurate measurements
    Are also a must.

MICHIGAN ROCKS

1 ½ c. sugar
2 eggs
3 c. flour or until stiff
1 tsp. baking soda
1 tsp. baking powder
1 tsp. cinnamon
1 tsp. cloves
½ tsp. allspice
1 lb. dates
1 c. margarine
½ c. milk
1 c. grapes
1 c. maraschino cherries
1 c. raisins
1 c. nuts
1 tsp. vanilla

Mix together and drop on a cookie sheet. Bake at 350° until done.

(Vern) Mary Ann Paul

CHOCOLATE SCOTCHEROOS

1 c. sugar
1 c. light corn syrup
1 c. peanut butter
6 c. Rice Krispies
1 (6 oz.) pkg. semi-sweet chocolate bits
1 (6 oz.) pkg. butterscotch bits

Combine sugar and corn syrup in saucepan. Cook over moderate heat, stirring frequently, until mixture begins to bubble. Remove from heat. Stir in peanut butter and mix well. Add Rice Krispies and mix. Press into buttered 13 x 9 x 2-inch pan. Melt chocolate and butterscotch bits in top of double boiler over hot water. Pour over Rice Krispies mixture. Cool until firm.

Rachel Esh

BUTTERSCOTCH MACAROONS

First Part:

2 egg whites
2 Tbsp. water
1 c. sugar
2 tsp. vanilla
4 c. flaked coconut
12 oz. butterscotch bits

Second Part:

1 c. butter or soft margarine
1 c. brown sugar
½ tsp. salt
3 c. sifted flour
1 tsp. soda

First Part: Beat egg whites with water until soft mounds form. Add vanilla. Stir into the coconut. Let stand and chill.

Second Part: Cream butter. Add brown sugar and egg yolks. Cream well. Add rest of vanilla and salt. Add flour and soda. Form in rolls and chill. Bake at 350°.

Rachel Esh

DATE PECAN BALLS

1 c. soft butter
½ c. sugar
2 tsp. vanilla
2 c. sifted flour
2 c. ground pecans
1 c. whole dates, cut up

Cream butter and sugar. Add vanilla and mix. Add flour and mix. Blend in pecans and dates. Roll teaspoonfuls of dough into balls.

Refrigerate balls for 1 to 2 hours. Bake at 350° on greased cookie sheet for approximately 20 minutes. Remove from oven and roll balls into powdered sugar. Sprinkle them again with powdered sugar after cookies have cooled.

Sara Stoltzfoos

CHOCOLATE CHIP COOKIES

2 ½ c. brown sugar
4 c. shortening
2 ½ c. white sugar
8 eggs
1 Tbsp. hot water
4 tsp. salt
4 tsp. soda
4 tsp. vanilla
10 c. flour
6 pkg. chocolate chips
4 c. nuts

Cream together the brown sugar, shortening, white sugar and eggs. Add and mix well the hot water, salt, soda and vanilla. Add the flour and mix well with the chocolate chips and nuts. Bake at 375° for 10 to 12 minutes. (This is a large go.)

Katie King
Liz Stoltzfus
(Hammertown)

CHOCOLATE CHIP COOKIES

2 ¼ c. flour
1 tsp. baking soda
1 tsp. salt
1 c. butter, softened
¾ c. sugar
¾ c. brown sugar
1 tsp. vanilla
2 eggs
2 c. chocolate chips

Preheat oven to 375°. In small bowl combine flour, baking soda and salt. Set aside. In large bowl combine butter, sugar, brown sugar and vanilla. Beat until creamy. Beat in eggs gradually and flour mixture. Mix well.

Naomi Grace Zook
Mrs. Edna B. Zook

SOFT CHOCOLATE CHIP COOKIES

3 c. brown sugar
1 c. butter flavor shortening or margarine
2 eggs
1 can evaporated milk
1 tsp. soda
1 Tbsp. vinegar
3 tsp. baking powder
1 Tbsp. vanilla
5 c. flour
2 ½ c. chocolate chips

Elsie Kauffman

CHOCOLATE CHIP COOKIES

2 c. butter
2 c. white sugar
2 c. brown sugar
4 eggs, beaten
2 tsp. vanilla
1 ½ tsp. soda, dissolved in 2 tsp. hot water
6 c. flour
2 tsp. salt
12 oz. pkg. chocolate chips

Cream shortening and sugars. Add beaten eggs and vanilla. Mix soda water alternately with flour sifted with salt. Add chips. Drop by teaspoon on greased cookie sheet. Bake 10 to 12 minutes in 375° oven.

I use pure sweet sugar. It makes moist and chewy cookies.

Barbara King

TOLL HOUSE COOKIES

1 ½ c. flour
1 tsp. soda
1 tsp. salt
1 c. shortening (½ oleo and ½ Crisco)
¾ c. brown sugar
¾ c. granulated sugar
2 eggs
1 tsp. hot water
1 c. nuts
2 pkg. chocolate chips
2 c. oatmeal
1 tsp. vanilla

Sift flour once before measuring. Sift with soda and salt. Cream shortening until soft. Add sugars gradually, creaming until soft and fluffy. Add eggs one at a time, beating each in. Add hot water to creamed mixture. Sift dry ingredients. Add nuts, chocolate chips and oatmeal. Mix thoroughly. Add vanilla and blend well. Bake at 300° to 375° for 8 minutes.

Fannie Glick

CHOCOLATE CHIP COOKIES

1 c. Wesson oil
½ c. sugar
1 c. brown sugar
1 tsp. vanilla
2 well beaten eggs
3 ¼ c. flour
1 tsp. salt
1 tsp. soda
1 c. chocolate chips

Cream the oil, sugars and vanilla. Add the eggs and beat until fluffy. Sift the flour, salt and soda. Add to creamed mixture and add chocolate chips. Bake at 375°.

Naomi Petersheim

HARD MOLASSES COOKIES

3 c. oil
4 c. brown sugar
½ c. Brer Rabbit molasses
½ c. regular molasses
4 eggs
8 tsp. soda
2 tsp. cloves
2 tsp. salt
2 tsp. ginger
10 c. flour
4 tsp. cinnamon

Bake in a moderate oven.

Barbie Zook

MOLASSES CRINKLES

1 ½ c. shortening
2 c. brown sugar
2 eggs
½ c. Brer Rabbit molasses
4 ½ c. flour
1 tsp. salt
2 tsp. cinnamon
1 tsp. ginger
1 tsp. cloves
4 tsp. soda

Cream shortening and sugar. Add eggs and molasses. Beat until well blended. Sift flour and spices. Add to creamed mixture and mix well. Chill dough in refrigerator. Shape chilled dough in balls and roll in granulated sugar. Flatten with fork. Bake at 350° for 12 to 15 minutes.

Ruth Stoltzfus

MOLASSES COOKIES

2 c. gold label Brer Rabbit molasses
1 c. butter or lard
1 ½ c. brown sugar
2 eggs
1 ½ c. sweet milk
4 tsp. soda
1 Tbsp. ginger
1 Tbsp. cinnamon
8 c. flour

Cream shortening and sugar. Add eggs and molasses. Sift dry ingredients and add alternately with milk. Bake in a 350° to 400° oven. Do not overbake. Spread white icing on top.

Anna King
Ruth Stoltzfus

SOFT MOLASSES COOKIES

5 to 6 c. sifted flour
3 tsp. soda
1 tsp. salt
2 tsp. ginger
3 tsp. cinnamon
1 c. shortening
2 c. brown sugar
2 eggs, beaten
1 c. Brer Rabbit molasses
2 c. sour milk or evaporated milk
1 tsp. vanilla

421792

Sift dry ingredients together 3 times. Cream other ingredients. Add flour with milk. Chill. Bake at 400° for 10 to 12 minutes.

Sylvia Stoltzfus
Barbie Zook

SPARKLING GINGERSNAPS

2 c. flour
2 tsp. soda
½ tsp. salt
½ tsp. cinnamon
¼ tsp. cloves
¼ tsp. ginger
¾ c. butter or margarine
1 c. sugar
1 unbeaten egg
¼ c. molasses

Mix together the flour, soda, salt, cinnamon, cloves and ginger. Cream the butter or margarine and sugar. Add the egg and molasses. Shape dough in balls. Roll in sugar. Place on ungreased cookie sheet. Bake at 375° for 9 to 12 minutes.

Priscilla King
Susie King

MOLASSES COOKIES

6 c. sifted flour
3 tsp. soda
1 tsp. salt
1 tsp. ginger
2 tsp. cinnamon
1 c. shortening
2 c. brown sugar
2 eggs, unbeaten
1 c. Brer Rabbit molasses
2 c. sour milk
1 tsp. vanilla

Sift dry ingredients together. Add flour with the milk and bake at 400° for 10 to 12 minutes.

Priscilla King

OATMEAL COOKIES

4 c. oatmeal
2 c. brown sugar
1 c. shortening
2 eggs
1 c. coconut
2 c. flour
1 tsp. soda
½ tsp. baking powder

Mix sugar, eggs and shortening. Add soda and powder. Add oatmeal and coconut. Gradually add flour.

Priscilla Fisher

CEREAL COCONUT COOKIES

1 c. shortening
1 c. granulated sugar
1 c. brown sugar
2 eggs
1 tsp. vanilla
2 c. oatmeal
2 c. Rice Krispies
1 c. coconut
2 c. flour
1 tsp. soda
½ tsp. baking powder

Cream the shortening and sugars together and add the eggs and vanilla. Add the remaining ingredients. Mix well. Take about 1 tablespoon cookie dough, press together and form round cookies. Place on cookie sheets. Bake 8 to 10 minutes at 375°.

Priscilla Fisher

BONBON COOKIES

1 c. butter
1 ½ c. 10x sugar
1 egg, beaten
1 tsp. vanilla
2 ½ c. flour
1 tsp. soda
1 tsp. cream of tartar

Chill overnight. Shape cookies about the size of a quarter. Put walnut on top. Bake at 350°.

Mary Stoltzfus

CHOCOLATE WHOOPIE PIES

½ c. shortening (oil)
1 c. brown sugar
2 eggs
1 ½ c. flour (½ all-purpose and ½ bread flour)
½ tsp. salt
1 tsp. soda
½ c. cocoa
½ c. milk
1 tsp. vanilla

Cream shortening, sugar and eggs. Add vanilla. Add milk with dry ingredients. Bake at 350° for 8 to 10 minutes.

Fannie Glick

WHOOPIE PIE FILLING

2 egg whites
2 tsp. vanilla
4 Tbsp. flour
2 Tbsp. milk
1 ½ c. shortening
1 lb. 10x sugar

Beat egg whites until stiff. Add vanilla, flour and milk. Beat well and add shortening and sugar.

Naomi Petersheim

WHOOPIE PIES

4 c. flour
2 c. sugar
2 tsp. soda
½ tsp. salt
1 c. shortening
1 c. cocoa
2 eggs
2 tsp. vanilla
1 c. thick sour milk
1 c. cold water

Cream together sugar, salt, shortening, vanilla and eggs. Sift together flour, soda and cocoa. Add this to the first mixture alternately with water and sour milk. Add slightly more flour if milk is not thick. Bake at 400°.

Naomi Petersheim
Sylvia Petersheim
Mrs. Edna B. Zook

PUMPKIN WHOOPIES

2 c. pumpkin
2 egg yolks
2 c. brown sugar
1 c. vegetable oil
1 tsp. cloves
1 tsp. ginger
1 tsp. salt
1 tsp. baking powder
1 tsp. soda
1 tsp. vanilla
3 c. flour

Filling:

2 egg whites
2 tsp. vanilla
4 Tbsp. flour
1 ½ c. vegetable shortening
2 Tbsp. milk
1 lb. 10x sugar

Mix together pumpkin, egg yolks, brown sugar, vegetable oil and vanilla until creamy. Sift and add dry ingredients. Bake at 375°.

Susie King
Katie King
Rachel Esh

OATMEAL WHOOPIE PIES

2 c. brown sugar
¾ c. butter
2 eggs
½ tsp. salt
2 c. flour
2 c. oatmeal
1 tsp. cinnamon
1 tsp. baking powder
2 tsp. soda, in 3 Tbsp. boiling water

Combine all ingredients. Add soda and water last. Bake at 350°.

Naomi Petersheim
Rachel Esh
Aarianne Petersheim

SAND TARTS

1 ½ c. white sugar
1 ½ c. brown sugar
1 ½ c. oil
1 c. butter
8 c. flour
3 egg yolks (save whites)
2 tsp. cinnamon
1 ½ tsp. soda

Roll all but egg whites in rolls. Chill overnight. Beat whites and brush on cookies when making. Makes 5 or 6 dozen.

Aarianne Petersheim

SAND TARTS

2 c. granulated sugar
2 c. brown sugar
4 c. flour (add flour last)
2 ½ c. lard
6 egg yolks
2 tsp. salt

Roll thin. Wash with egg white. Sprinkle with cinnamon or sugar.

Katie S. King

GRANDMOTHER KING'S SAND TARTS

1 ½ c. brown sugar
1 ¼ c. granulated sugar
4 c. flour
1 c. plus 2 oz. butter
3 egg yolks
1 tsp. soda

Roll out and cut. Bake at 350° about 8 minutes or until a little brown. You can sprinkle on sugar. Decorate however you want.

Priscilla King

DROP SAND TARTS

¼ lb. butter
1 lb. sugar (2 c.)
3 eggs
1 tsp. milk
pinch of baking soda
1 lb. flour (4 c.)

421792

Add baking soda to the milk. Mix butter and sugar with your hands. Beat eggs. Add soda mixture and butter mixture and then your sifted flour. Drop by teaspoon on greased baking sheet. Brush with beaten egg and top with cinnamon. Bake in a 350° oven until light brown.

Priscilla King

MONSTER COOKIES

12 eggs
4 c. white sugar
4 c. brown sugar
⅓ c. vanilla
8 tsp. soda
1 lb. M&M's
2 c. nuts
1 lb. butter (do not substitute)
3 lb. peanut butter
18 c. oatmeal
1 lb. chocolate chips

Mix in order given. Bake at 350°.

Fannie Glick

PEANUT BUTTER COOKIES

½ c. butter
½ c. peanut butter
½ c. sugar
½ c. brown sugar
1 egg
1 ¼ c. flour, sifted
½ tsp. baking powder
¾ tsp. baking soda
¼ tsp. salt

Mix thoroughly and roll in balls the size of walnuts. Place on cookie sheets. Flatten in a crisscross pattern with fork dipped in flour. Bake until set, but not hard at 375° for 10 to 12 minutes.

Sylvia Petersheim

PEANUT BUTTER COOKIES

1 c. shortening
1 c. peanut butter
1 c. brown sugar
1 c. white sugar
2 eggs
3 c. flour
½ tsp. salt
2 tsp. soda
1 tsp. baking powder
1 tsp. vanilla

Bake at 375°.

Naomi Petersheim

PEANUT BUTTER COOKIES

2 c. peanut butter
1 c. butter
2 c. sugar
1 c. brown sugar
2 tsp. soda
2 tsp. vanilla
8 Tbsp. water
4 c. flour

Cream butter, peanut butter and sugar. Mix well. Add soda, vanilla, water and flour. Dough will be dry. Roll in long strip rolls. Refrigerate ½ hour. Cut ½-inch thick. Press with fork. Bake at 350° for 10 to 12 minutes.

P.S. Let set on hot cookie sheet 1 to 2 minutes or they will crumble.

Susie King

DOUBLE TREAT COOKIES

2 c. flour
2 tsp. baking soda
½ tsp. salt
1 c. lard
1 c. granulated sugar
1 c. brown sugar
1 tsp. vanilla
2 eggs
1 c. peanut butter
6 oz. chocolate chips
6 oz. chopped nuts

Bake at 350° for 10 to 12 minutes. Easy to make.

Susie S. King

CHOCOLATE PEANUT BUTTER COOKIES

1 c. Crisco
2 sticks butter
1 ½ c. brown sugar
1 ½ c. granulated sugar
4 eggs
1 ½ tsp. soda
1 tsp. salt
⅔ c. cocoa
2 tsp. vanilla
4 c. flour
1 (12 oz.) bag peanut butter chips

Bake at 350°.

Fannie Riehl

PEANUT BUTTER TREATS

1 c. butter, soft
1 c. brown sugar
1 c. granulated sugar
2 eggs
1 c. peanut butter
1 tsp. vanilla
2 ½ c. flour
1 ¼ tsp. soda
1 tsp. salt

Combine sugars, butter, eggs, peanut butter and vanilla. Beat until smooth. In a separate bowl combine flour, baking soda and salt. Add to creamed mixture. Chill dough. When cold enough to handle easily, roll in small (walnut size) balls. Place each ball in greased miniature muffin tins. Bake at 375° for 8 to 9 minutes. Remove from oven. Press 1 peanut butter cup into each cookie.

Fannie Riehl

PEANUT BUTTER OATMEAL COOKIES

- 1 c. shortening, soft
- 1 c. firmly packed brown sugar
- ¾ c. granulated sugar
- 2 eggs
- 1 c. creamy peanut butter
- 2 c. sifted all-purpose flour
- 2 tsp. soda
- ½ tsp. salt
- 1 c. Quaker oats (quick or old fashioned), uncooked

Beat shortening and sugars together until creamy. Add eggs and peanut butter. Beat well. Sift together flour, soda and salt. Add to creamed mixture, mixing well. Stir in oats. Shape dough to form 1-inch balls. Place on ungreased cookie sheets. With tines of fork, press to make a crisscross on each. (If dough sticks to fork, occasionally dip fork in flour.) Bake in preheated moderate oven (350°) for 8 to 10 minutes. Makes 6 dozen.

Rachel Esh

PEANUT BUTTER BLOSSOMS

- 1 c. shortening
- 1 ½ c. peanut butter
- ⅔ c. sugar
- ⅔ c. packed brown sugar
- 2 eggs
- 4 Tbsp. milk
- 2 tsp. vanilla
- 2 ⅔ c. unsifted all-purpose flour
- 2 tsp. baking soda
- 1 tsp. salt
- granulated sugar
- 1 (8 oz.) pkg. Hershey's Kisses

Cream shortening and peanut butter. Add sugar and brown sugar. Add eggs, milk and vanilla. Beat well. Combine flour, baking soda and salt. Gradually add to creamed mixture, blending thoroughly. Shape dough into 1-inch balls. Roll in granulated sugar. Place on ungreased cookie sheet. Bake at 375° for 10 to 12 minutes. Remove from oven. Immediately place unwrapped Kiss on top of each cookie, pressing down so that cookie cracks around edge. Remove from cookie sheet. Cool. Makes about 4 dozen cookies.

Rachel Esh
Barbie Zook

BROWN SUGAR COOKIES

4 c. brown sugar
2 c. Wesson oil
8 eggs, unbeaten
1 can evaporated milk
7 c. flour
4 tsp. soda
2 tsp. baking powder
2 Tbsp. vanilla
½ tsp. salt

Cream the sugar and oil. Add remaining ingredients.

Rachel King

DATE FILLED COOKIES

Filling:

¾ c. sugar
¾ c. pitted dates
¾ c. water
⅜ tsp. vanilla

Cook sugar, dates and water together until thick, then add vanilla.

Dough:

⅜ c. butter
1 ½ c. sifted flour
1 ½ c. quick oatmeal
1 c. brown sugar
1 tsp. soda
2 tsp. baking powder
4 Tbsp. milk

Mix as for pie dough and wet with milk. Cut with round cookie cutter. Place teaspoon of filling on one disk and top with another. Bake on ungreased cookie sheet about 15 minutes at 375°.

Rachel King

SAND TART COOKIES

1 lb. sugar
1 c. brown sugar
1 c. white sugar
1 lb. flour (4 c.)
9 oz. lard
3 egg yolks
1 tsp. soda (heaping)

Wash with white of egg. Sprinkle with 10x sugar, cinnamon and nuts. Bake at 350°.

Rachel King

421792

ROCKY ROAD DROP COOKIES

1 ½ c. butter
1 ⅔ c. brown sugar
3 tsp. vanilla
3 eggs
1 ½ c. semi-sweet chocolate morsels, melted
1 ½ tsp. soda
¾ tsp. salt
3 tsp. instant coffee
1 c. milk
marshmallow halves, cut with scissors dipped in water
4 ½ c. flour
½ c. walnuts (optional)

Cream butter and brown sugar. Stir in vanilla, eggs and chocolate. Add dry ingredients. Chill dough. Drop on cookie sheet and bake at 450° for 8 minutes. Put marshmallow halves on top of cookies (cut side down). Return to oven until marshmallows are soft (1 to 2 minutes).

Chocolate Icing:

½ c. butter
½ c. milk
1 c. chocolate chips
½ tsp. salt
2 tsp. vanilla
5 c. powdered sugar

Melt butter and chocolate chips. Stir in milk and add dry ingredients.

Rachel King

POOR MAN'S COOKIES

1 c. raisins
1 ½ c. water
2 Tbsp. Crisco
1 c. sugar
2 c. flour
1 tsp. baking powder
1 tsp. soda
½ tsp. nutmeg
1 c. 10x sugar
enough water to make syrup

Stew the raisins in the water. Add more water to make 1 cup juice after being stewed. Add Crisco and cool. Sift and add the sugar, flour, baking powder, soda and nutmeg. Spread on jelly roll pan. Bake at 375° for 18 to 20 minutes. Mix the 10x sugar and enough water to make a syrup and pour over cake while cake is still warm. (Not hot or syrup will soak in.) When cool, cut into bars.

Nancy Ann Esch

SUGAR COOKIES

2 c. Crisco
8 eggs, beaten
4 c. brown sugar
4 tsp. soda
2 tsp. baking powder
2 c. milk
1 tsp. vanilla
7 to 8 c. flour

Sprinkle cookies with sugar before baking. Use half white sugar and half brown sugar.

Liz Stoltzfus

SUGAR COOKIES

1 lb. lard
2 lb. brown sugar
8 eggs
2 c. evaporated milk
7 to 8 c. flour
4 tsp. soda
2 tsp. baking powder
vanilla and salt

Bake at 400°. Add icing and nuts.

Naomi Petersheim

SNOWBALLS

1 c. butter
¼ c. sugar
2 c. ground nuts
2 c. sifted flour
10x sugar

Cream butter. Add sugar, nuts and flour and mix well. Make balls using about 1 tablespoon of dough for cookie. Bake at 300° on ungreased sheets 45 minutes. Roll in 10x sugar or donut sugar when first taken from oven, then cool and roll in sugar again.

Susie S. King

PUMPKIN COOKIES

1 c. lard
1 c. pumpkin
1 tsp. cinnamon
1 tsp. baking powder
1 egg
1 c. brown sugar
2 c. flour
1 tsp. soda
½ tsp. salt

Mix together sugar, lard and egg. Add pumpkin. Mix well. Add dry ingredients to mixture and beat well. Drop on cookie sheet and bake at 350° for 10 to 20 minutes. Cover with icing.

Mrs. Elam Z. Stoltzfus

RAISIN COOKIES

2 c. raisins
1 c. boiling water
1 c. shortening
2 c. sugar
3 eggs
1 tsp. vanilla
4 c. flour
1 tsp. baking powder
1 tsp. soda
1 tsp. salt
¼ tsp. nutmeg
¼ tsp. cloves
1 tsp. cinnamon

Add boiling water to raisins and cook for 5 minutes. Cool. Cream shortening and sugar together. Add eggs and vanilla and beat until fluffy. Add cooled raisins to creamed mixture and mix thoroughly. Sift together flour, salt, soda, baking powder and spices. Mix well. Bake at 350°.

Elizabeth Stoltzfus

OATMEAL RAISIN COOKIES

3 eggs, well beaten
1 tsp. vanilla
1 c. raisins
1 c. shortening
1 c. brown sugar
2 ½ c. flour
1 tsp. salt
2 tsp. soda
1 tsp. cinnamon
2 c. oatmeal
1 c. chopped nuts (optional)

In a large mixing bowl, stir together all ingredients. Shape into 1-inch balls. Place on ungreased baking sheets. Flatten with fingers. Bake at 350° for 10 to 11 minutes or until golden brown. Do not overbake.

Linda Fisher

RAISIN MOLASSES GEMS

¾ c. shortening
1 c. sugar
¼ c. molasses
1 egg
2 c. flour
1 c. raisins
2 tsp. soda
1 tsp. cinnamon
½ tsp. cloves
½ tsp. ginger
¼ tsp. salt

Beat shortening and 1 cup sugar until light and fluffy. Add molasses and egg. Beat well. Combine flour, soda, cinnamon, cloves, ginger and salt. Add to molasses mixture. Mix well. Stir in raisins.

Cover. Refrigerate until chilled. Shape into balls and roll in sugar. Bake at 350°. Makes 3 dozen.

Naomi Grace Zook

SOFT RAISIN OATMEAL COOKIES

1 c. brown sugar
1 c. granulated sugar
1 c. butter or margarine
3 ¼ c. flour
1 egg
1 c. milk
1 c. oatmeal
1 ½ c. raisins
1 tsp. soda
1 tsp. vanilla

Cream sugar and butter. Add egg and milk. Mix well. Add rest of ingredients. Bake at 350°.

Nancy Ann Esch

PUMPKIN COOKIES

1 ½ c. white sugar
¾ c. shortening
1 egg
1 ½ c. pumpkin
1 tsp. vanilla
3 ½ c. flour
1 ½ tsp. baking soda
1 tsp. salt
1 tsp. nutmeg
1 ½ tsp. cinnamon
½ tsp. ginger
½ tsp. cloves
1 c. nuts (optional)

Cream the sugar, shortening, egg, pumpkin and vanilla together. Add the remaining ingredients and bake. Put icing on.

Icing:

½ c. brown sugar
3 Tbsp. butter
¼ c. milk
2 c. 10x sugar
1 tsp. vanilla

Boil the brown sugar, butter and milk for 2 minutes. Cool. Beat in the powdered sugar and vanilla.

Susie Smucker

CHOCOLATE-CHERRY NUT DROP COOKIES

2 ½ c. flour
1 tsp. baking soda
½ tsp. salt
1 c. margarine
1 c. brown sugar
½ c. sugar
1 egg, unbeaten
1 ½ tsp. vanilla
1 c. chocolate chips
½ c. chopped nuts
¼ c. chopped maraschino cherries

Sift together the flour, baking soda and salt. Cream the margarine and gradually add the brown sugar and sugar. Blend in the egg and vanilla. Add dry ingredients gradually, blending well. Stir in the chocolate chips, chopped nuts and cherries. Drop by rounded teaspoonfuls onto greased cookie sheet. Bake at 350° until done.

(Vern) Mary Ann Paul

HAPPY HOME RECIPE

4 c. love
2 c. loyalty
3 c. forgiveness
1 c. friendship
5 spoons hope
2 spoons tenderness
4 qt. faith
1 barrel laughter

Take love and loyalty. Mix it thoroughly with faith. Blend it with tenderness, kindness and understanding. Add friendship and hope. Sprinkle abundantly with laughter. Bake it with sunshine. Serve daily with generous helpings.

Priscilla King

BROWNIES

¾ c. oleo or butter
½ c. brown sugar
½ c. white sugar
3 eggs, separated
1 tsp. vanilla
2 c. flour
1 tsp. baking powder
½ tsp. salt
¼ tsp. soda

Dough will be very stiff. Spread thin on shallow cake pan. Beat egg whites until frothy. Add 1 cup brown sugar and make stiff. Put on top. Sprinkle with nuts, chocolate chips or coconut. Bake at 350° for 35 to 40 minutes.

Aarianne Petersheim
Fannie Glick
Liz Stoltzfus

FUDGE BROWNIES

1 ½ c. flour
1 tsp. salt
2 c. sugar
½ c. cocoa
2 tsp. vanilla
1 c. oil
1 c. chopped nuts
4 eggs
¼ c. cold water

Put all ingredients in beater bowl in order given and beat on low speed. Do not beat too long. Bake at 350° for 30 minutes (no longer) in a 13 x 9 x 2-inch pan (not smaller).

Icing:

2 sq. unsweetened chocolate
1 c. 4x sugar
1 egg, beaten
2 tsp. butter
1 tsp. vanilla

Melt the chocolate in double boiler and stir into it the 4x sugar, egg, butter and vanilla. Remove from heat at once. Stir. Cool a little before spreading.

Naomi King

HERSHEY DOUBLE CHOCOLATE MINT

1 c. flour
1 c. sugar
½ c. butter, softened
4 eggs
1 ½ c. Hershey's syrup

Mix and pour into a 13 x 9 x 2-inch pan. Bake at 350° for 25 to 30 minutes. Let cool.

Mint Cream Layer:

2 c. 10x sugar
½ c. margarine
1 Tbsp. vanilla
½ tsp. mint extract
3 drops green food coloring

Mix and put on top of cooled cake.

Chocolate Topping:

6 Tbsp. margarine
1 c. Hershey's mint chocolate chips

Melt and pour on top.

Anna Fisher

MILK CHOCOLATE BROWNIES

½ c. butter
2 c. sugar
4 eggs
1 ½ c. flour
½ c. cocoa
½ tsp. salt
1 c. coconut

Melt butter. Add sugar and eggs. Add dry ingredients. Mix well. Stir in coconut. Spread in a 9 x 13-inch pan.

Topping:

½ c. chocolate chips
2 Tbsp. sugar
½ c. chopped walnuts

Bake at 350° for 25 minutes.

Fannie Riehl

BROWNIES
(Good and Easy Bar)

⅓ c. margarine
¾ c. sugar
⅓ c. honey
2 tsp. vanilla
½ c. unsifted all-purpose flour
½ c. cocoa
1 c. nuts

Cream margarine and sugar. Blend in honey and vanilla. Add eggs, one at a time, beating well each time. Combine flour and cocoa and gradually add to the creamed mixture. Stir in the nuts. Bake in a 9-inch baking dish for 25 to 30 minutes at 350°.

Priscilla King

CHOCOLATE CHIP COOKIE BARS

1 ½ c. soft margarine
4 ½ c. brown sugar
6 eggs
3 tsp. vanilla
4 ½ c. flour
4 ½ tsp. baking powder
1 ½ tsp. salt
2 c. chocolate chips or butterscotch chips
½ c. nuts

This makes 2 (9 x 13-inch) cake pans full. Bake at 325°.

Rachel Esh

PEEK-A-BOO SQUARES

2 sticks oleo
2 c. sugar
1 tsp. vanilla
1 tsp. almond extract or 2 tsp. vanilla
4 eggs, one at a time
2 ¾ c. flour

Cream the oleo and sugar together well. Add the vanilla and almond extract or 2 teaspoons of vanilla. Add the eggs, one at a time. Alternately add the flour. Place ¾ of the batter on greased cookie sheet with sides. Pour on any flavor pie filling. Dot rest of batter on top. Bake at 350° for 25 to 40 minutes.

(Vern) Mary Ann Paul

RAISIN BARS
(High Fiber Recipe)

1 c. raisins
1 c. water
⅓ c. oil
½ c. molasses or ¼ c. brown sugar
1 egg
1 c. whole wheat flour
½ c. chopped nuts
¾ c. rolled oats
1 tsp. cinnamon
1 tsp. soda
1 tsp. allspice
½ tsp. cloves
¼ tsp. salt

Bring the raisins and water to a boil. Remove from heat and add oil and molasses or brown sugar. When cool, add egg. Mix the dry ingredients, then add the two mixtures together. Bake at 375° for 20 minutes.

Aarianne Petersheim

CHOCOLATE CHIP CHEWS

⅔ c. oil
½ c. sugar
½ c. brown sugar
3 eggs
1 tsp. vanilla
1 tsp. salt
½ tsp. baking powder
½ tsp. soda
2 ½ c. flour
1 c. chocolate chips

Bake at 350° for 20 minutes. Take out of oven when they look hardly done.

Aarianne Petersheim

RASPBERRY BARS

¾ c. margarine
1 c. brown sugar
1 ½ c. flour
1 tsp. salt
½ tsp. soda
1 ½ c. oats, uncooked
1 (10 oz.) jar red raspberry preserves

Cream margarine and sugar until light and fluffy. Add combined dry ingredients and mix well. Press half of crumb mixture into greased 9 x 13-inch pan. Spread with preserves and sprinkle with remaining crumb mixture. Bake at 400° for 20 to 25 minutes. Cool and cut into bars.

Liz Stoltzfus

RUTHIE TIRAM TROOP BROWNIES

¾ c. butter
½ c. brown sugar
½ c. granulated sugar
3 egg yolks
1 tsp. vanilla
2 c. flour
1 tsp. baking powder
¼ tsp. salt

Top Part:

egg whites
1 c. brown sugar

Make like a meringue. Spread on top. Sprinkle with nuts, tiny peanut butter bits and tiny chocolate chips. Bake 15 minutes at 350°, then at 325° the next 15 minutes.

Susie S. King

CHOCOLATE CHIP MERINGUE BARS

1 c. margarine
½ c. granulated sugar
½ c. brown sugar
2 c. flour
3 egg yolks
3 Tbsp. water
1 tsp. baking powder
¼ tsp. baking soda
¼ tsp. salt
1 tsp. vanilla

Put batter in flat cookie sheet. Spread out evenly. Put 2 cups chocolate chips on top of batter, then top with 3 egg whites, stiffly beaten. Add ½ cup brown sugar to egg whites. Bake at 350° for 30 to 35 minutes.

Susie S. King

ROCKY ROAD CHOCOLATE BARS

2 sq. chocolate
2 sticks butter (1 c.)
4 eggs
2 c. sugar
1 ½ c. flour
1 tsp. baking powder
½ tsp. salt
1 tsp. vanilla
2 c. miniature marshmallows
1 c. chopped nuts

Melt chocolate and butter. Cool. Beat eggs and sugar until light. Add cooled chocolate mixture. Mix in dry ingredients. Last add vanilla, nuts and marshmallows. Bake at 350° for 30 minutes in an 11 x 15-inch pan.

Substitute: Use scant ½ cup cocoa instead of chocolate and 1 ¼ cups vegetable oil instead of butter. Do not heat. Add to egg and sugar mixture.

Linda Fisher

ROCKY ROAD BARS

1 c. butter
1 c. 10x sugar
2 eggs
2 c. chocolate chips

Melt ingredients in double boiler. Remove from heat. Add 4 cups marshmallows. Line a 9 x 13 x 2-inch pan with graham crackers. Pour mixture on top. Cool and cut in bars.

Priscilla King

RHUBARB SQUARES

1 ½ c. brown sugar
½ c. shortening
1 egg
2 c. Pillsbury flour
1 tsp. soda
½ tsp. salt
1 c. sour milk
1 ½ c. rhubarb

Topping:

½ c. granulated sugar
1 Tbsp. melted butter
1 tsp. cinnamon
½ c. chopped nuts (optional)

Susie Smucker

CREAM CHEESE BARS

5 Tbsp. butter
1 block chocolate (1 oz.)
scant ¾ c. sugar
2 eggs
⅔ c. flour
½ tsp. salt
½ tsp. baking powder
1 tsp. vanilla
8 oz. cream cheese
scant ½ c. sugar
1 tsp. vanilla
1 egg

Melt the butter and chocolate. Add the ¾ cup sugar, 2 eggs, flour, salt, baking powder and vanilla. Mix together and put into a cake pan. Mix together the cream cheese, ½ cup sugar, vanilla and 1 egg. Pour on top of chocolate mixture. Sprinkle with chocolate chips and nuts, if desired. Swirl with a knife and bake at 350° for 20 minutes.

Elizabeth Stoltzfus

BLONDE BROWNIES

⅔ c. butter
2 ½ c. brown sugar
3 eggs
2 ½ tsp. baking powder
½ tsp. salt
½ c. chocolate chips
2 ⅔ c. flour

Mix and spread in a 9 x 13-inch pan. Bake at 350° for 30 minutes.

Fannie Riehl

M&M BARS

2 c. oatmeal
1 ½ c. flour
1 c. brown sugar
1 tsp. soda
¾ tsp. salt
1 c. margarine, melted
1 can sweetened condensed milk
⅓ c. peanut butter
1 c. M&M's

Combine oats, flour, sugar, soda and salt. Add margarine. Mix until dry ingredients are moist. Reserve 1 cup crumbs. Press remaining mixture into bottom of a 9 x 13-inch pan. Bake at 350° for 12 minutes. Combine condensed milk and peanut butter in small bowl. Spread over partially baked crust. Combine reserved crumbs and candies. Sprinkle on top, pressing lightly. Bake 20 minutes longer.

Fannie Riehl

LEMON SUPREME

1 c. walnuts
1 c. flour
¼ lb. butter
1 c. Cool Whip
8 oz. cream cheese
½ c. 10x
2 pkg. pudding (any flavor)

Mix the walnuts, flour and butter and bake 15 minutes. Combine the Cool Whip, cream cheese and 10x and spread on crust. Mix the pudding for the top. Let chill and garnish with Cool Whip and walnuts.

Aarianne Petersheim

LEMON BARS

Crust:

2 c. flour
1 c. margarine
½ c. 10x sugar

Mix and press in a 9 x 13-inch pan. Bake 20 minutes at 350°.

4 eggs
2 c. sugar
6 Tbsp. lemon juice
1 grated rind of lemon
¼ c. flour
1 tsp. baking powder

Mix and pour over crust. Bake another 25 minutes. Sprinkle with 10x sugar.

Aarianne Petersheim
Sylvia Stoltzfus
Susie King

FRUIT PIZZA

Crust:

2 ½ c. Bisquick
½ c. milk
3 Tbsp. sugar
3 Tbsp. butter

Filling:

8 oz. cream cheese
3 oz. marshmallow cream
a little orange juice

Bake 10 minutes at 425°. Arrange fruit and pour glaze over it.

Glaze:

⅔ c. sugar
2 Tbsp. cornstarch
¼ tsp. salt
1 Tbsp. orange juice

Naomi Petersheim

MINCE FRUIT PASTRY SQUARES

2 ½ c. sifted flour
1 Tbsp. sugar
1 Tbsp. salt
1 c. lard
1 egg, separated
milk
3 c. mince fruit filling
1 c. 10x sugar
2 Tbsp. lemon juice

Mix first 4 ingredients as for pie dough. Beat egg yolks in measuring cup and add milk to make ½ cup. Mix enough in dough to roll out. Roll out half of it and put on baking sheet. Spread with mince fruit filling. Roll out the rest of dough for top and seal edges. Spread with beaten egg whites. Bake at 400° for 25 to 30 minutes. Mix 10x sugar and lemon juice. Drizzle over top of crust while hot.

Rachel Esh

CREAM PUFFS

½ c. butter
1 c. boiling water
1 c. flour
4 eggs

In saucepan put butter in with boiling water and boil until butter is melted, then add flour all at once and really stir until mixture is smooth and doesn't stick to sides. Cool slightly. Add eggs, one at a time, until mixture is smooth. Drop with teaspoon on sheet and bake in hot oven at 400° for 35 minutes. Allow to cool before filling.

Filling:

1 ⅓ c. sugar
½ tsp. salt
10 Tbsp. flour
4 c. milk
4 eggs, beaten
2 tsp. vanilla

Put sugar, salt and flour in saucepan and slowly stir in milk. Boil and remove from heat. Stir in eggs and boil again. Add vanilla and cool.

Icing:

10x sugar, enough to taste sweet
1 c. shortening or lard
1 stick melted butter
½ c. peanut butter

Aarianne Petersheim

CRUNCH BARS

1 stick butter or margarine
¾ c. white sugar
2 eggs, beaten
¼ tsp. baking powder
¼ tsp. salt
1 c. flour
½ c. crushed walnuts (optional)

Bake at 325° for 20 minutes. Remove from oven and put 1 ½ cups miniature marshmallows on top of cake. Put in oven again until marshmallows are melted. Cool.

1 ½ c. chocolate chips
1 c. peanut butter
2 c. Rice Krispies

Melt the chocolate chips and peanut butter. Add the Rice Krispies. Put this on top of cake and cut into bars.

Elsie Kauffman
Liz Stoltzfus

GRANOLA BARS

3 ½ c. oatmeal
1 c. raisins
1 c. chopped nuts
⅔ c. melted butter
½ c. brown sugar
⅓ c. honey
⅓ c. corn syrup
⅓ c. molasses
1 egg, beaten
½ tsp. vanilla
½ tsp. salt

In a 350° oven for 15 to 20 minutes toast oats in ungreased 9 x 13-inch pan. Combine oats with remaining ingredients. Press firmly into well-greased pan. Do not bake. When cooled, cut into bars.

Rebecca K. Stoltzfus

GRANOLA BARS

1 ½ lb. marshmallows
¼ c. butter or margarine
¼ c. Wesson oil
½ c. honey
¼ c. peanut butter
9 ½ c. Rice Krispies
5 c. oatmeal
1 c. crushed peanuts
1 ½ c. raisins
1 c. coconut
1 c. graham crackers, crumbled into pieces
1 c. chocolate chips or M&M's

Melt the marshmallows and butter or margarine. Add the oil, honey and peanut butter. In another bowl combine the Rice

Krispies, oatmeal, crushed peanuts, raisins, coconut, graham crackers and chocolate chips or M&M's. Mix with marshmallow mixture. Pat into buttered cake pans and cool. Cut into bars.

Nancy Ann Esch

RECIPE FOR A LITTLE BOY

A chocolate bar
A ball thrown far
A box of junk
A mud, one hunk!
Five bugs, six rocks
And rubber bands
A sticky face
Two grimy hands
Such varied sounds
Of trucks and hounds
A scuffling fight
An appetite
A shrill of shouts
And ton of joy
One curious mind
One happy boy.

PEANUT BUTTER CANDY

2 c. peanut butter
½ c. soft or melted butter
2 ½ c. 10x sugar
½ c. brown sugar
½ tsp. vanilla
6 oz. chocolate bits or coating chocolate

Rachel Esh

BABY RUTH BARS

½ c. sugar
½ c. Karo
¾ c. crunchy peanut butter
3 c. Rice Krispies
6 oz. chocolate bits
3 oz. butterscotch bits

Bring the sugar and Karo to a boil. Add the peanut butter and Rice Krispies. Spread in greased pan. Melt the bits together and pour over top.

Aarianne Petersheim

PEANUT BUTTER CUPS

½ c. margarine
1 Tbsp. hot milk
2 c. Marshmallow Creme
2 Tbsp. Crisco
2 Tbsp. flour
1 Tbsp. vanilla
1 lb. 10x sugar
12 oz. peanut butter

Shape into balls and dip in chocolate.

Aarianne Petersheim

PEANUT BUTTER EGGS

1 lb. butter
18 oz. jar peanut butter plus 1 large Tbsp.
7 oz. jar Marshmallow Creme
1 ½ to 2 lb. 4x sugar

Beat butter until whipped. Add Marshmallow Creme and mix well. Add peanut butter and mix well. Add 1 pound of 4x sugar first, then rest of sugar slowly. Mix well. Shape in balls or eggs, then freeze before coating with chocolate. They handle nicer if frozen.

Ruth Stoltzfus

REESE BALLS

(Candy)

1 lb. butter or margarine, melted
2 lb. peanut butter
2 ½ lb. 10x sugar
3 tsp. vanilla

Mix all ingredients together. Roll in balls and chill. Dip in melted chocolate and store in cool place.

Katie King
Barbara King
Susie King

DATE NUT ROLL

1 lb. walnuts
2 (8 oz.) pkg. dates
1 lb. raisins
1 jar maraschino cherries and juice
1 pkg. miniature marshmallows
1 lb. 10x sugar
1 small can cream
2 or 3 pkg. graham cracker crumbs

Chop dates. Place cherries and juice, marshmallows and cream in large mixing bowl. Let soften a little. Rinse raisins in warm water.

421792

Combine all ingredients (1 ½ packages graham crumbs) and mix well. Roll into balls, then roll in rest of graham crumbs.

Barbara King

CREAMY-SURE FUDGE

(Candy)

- ⅔ c. evaporated milk (1 small can)
- 16 marshmallows or 1 c. Marshmallow Creme
- 1 ⅓ c. sugar
- ¼ c. butter or oleo
- ¼ tsp. salt
- 2 c. semi-sweet chocolate pieces
- 1 tsp. vanilla
- 1 c. coarsely chopped walnuts

Mix first 5 ingredients in saucepan, stirring constantly. Heat to boiling and boil 5 minutes only. Remove from heat. Add chocolate. Stir until melted. Stir in vanilla and walnuts. Spread in an 8-inch pan. Cool until firm.

Mrs. Edna B. Zook

DATE BALLS

- 1 lb. dates
- 1 c. sugar
- 2 eggs
- 4 Tbsp. butter
- 3 c. Rice Krispies
- 1 tsp. vanilla
- 1 c. chopped pecans

Heat the dates, sugar, eggs and butter for 7 minutes. Cool slightly. Add the remaining ingredients. Make balls. Roll in coconut.

Fannie Riehl

PUPPY CHOW

- 8 c. Corn Chex
- 1 c. semi-sweet chocolate chips
- 1 stick butter
- 1 c. peanut butter

Melt chocolate. Add butter. Mix well. Add peanut butter. Stir until mixed. Pour over Chex in large bowl. Cover and shake vigorously. When Chex are coated, add 2 cups 10x sugar. Put on lid and shake lightly until all Chex are white.

Fannie Riehl

CHRISTMAS CRISPIES

1 (6 oz.) pkg. butterscotch chips
½ c. peanut butter
5 c. Rice Krispies cereal

Stir chips and peanut butter in pan over low heat until melted. Pour mixture over cereal and stir, coating all. Drop by spoon on wax paper. Chill 2 hours.

Mae Gay
Brooks, OR

PEANUT BUTTER CANDY

1 lb. butter
2 lb. peanut butter
3 lb. 10x sugar
1 (8 oz.) cream cheese (if you wish)

Mix together until it gets stiff enough that you can mix it with your hands. Coat with chocolate.

Priscilla Fisher

CHOCOLATE SCOTCHEROOS

1 c. sugar
1 c. light corn syrup
1 c. peanut butter
6 c. Rice Krispies
1 (6 oz.) pkg. semi-sweet chocolate bits
1 (6 oz.) pkg. butterscotch bits

Combine sugar and corn syrup in saucepan. Cook over moderate heat, stirring frequently, until mixture begins to bubble. Remove from heat. Stir in peanut butter. Mix well. Add Rice Krispies and mix. Press into buttered 13 x 9 x 2-inch pan. Melt chocolate and butterscotch bits in top of double boiler over hot water. Pour over Rice Krispies mixture. Cool until firm.

Rachel Esh

TAFFY

4 c. sugar
1 pt. Karo
flavoring
1 pt. evaporated milk
paraffin, size of walnut

421792

Cook 15 minutes, then add 1 tablespoon gelatin soaked in ½ cup water. Cook until it gets hard enough to pull when put in cold water, then pour into buttered pan and cool. Pull.

Sylvia Stoltzfus
Nancy Ann Esch

JOY OF HAPPINESS

Joy is not in things. It is in us. Happiness is the product of right thinking and right acting, and there is no human being in the world who cannot be happy by complying with the law that produces happiness. It is a product that comes back to us from what we send out. No one ever found happiness who did not manufacture it for himself. It is product of our mental attitude toward others.

BAKED CUP CUSTARD

- 4 eggs
- ½ c. sugar
- ¼ tsp. salt
- 4 c. milk
- ½ tsp. vanilla

Beat eggs. Add sugar, salt and vanilla. Scald milk and add to mixture. Stir thoroughly. Pour into custard cups, filling ⅔ full. Sprinkle nutmeg. Set in hot water to bake. Bake at 400° for 10 minutes, then at 350° until done. Makes 8 custards.

Susie Smucker

PUMPKIN TORTE

- 24 graham crackers, crushed to about 3 c.
- ⅓ c. sugar
- ½ c. butter, melted
- 2 eggs
- ¾ c. sugar
- 1 (8 oz.) pkg. cream cheese
- 2 c. pumpkin
- 3 egg yolks
- ½ c. sugar
- ½ c. milk
- ½ tsp. salt
- 1 Tbsp. cinnamon
- 1 Tbsp. unflavored gelatin
- ¼ c. cold water
- 3 egg whites
- ¼ c. sugar

Mix grahams, ⅓ cup sugar and butter. Press into a 9 x 13-inch cake pan. Mix eggs, ¾ cup sugar and cream cheese and pour over crust. Bake 20 minutes at 350°. Cook pumpkin, egg yolks, ½ cup sugar, milk, salt and cinnamon until mixture thickens. Remove from heat. Add gelatin dissolved in ¼ cup cold water (cool). Beat egg whites and ¼ cup sugar and fold into pumpkin mixture. Pour over cooled baked crust and chill. Serve with whipped cream (optional).

Nancy Ann Esch

LEMON PUFF PUDDING

3 Tbsp. soft butter or margarine
1 c. granulated sugar
¼ c. all-purpose flour
3 eggs, separated
2 tsp. grated lemon rind
¼ c. lemon juice
1 ½ c. milk
¼ tsp. salt

Cream butter, ½ cup sugar and flour in mixing bowl. Add egg yolks. Beat well. Stir in lemon rind, juice and milk. Add salt to egg whites and beat until stiff. Gradually beat in remaining sugar. Fold into first mixture. Pour in 1 ½ quart buttered baking dish. Set dish in shallow pan containing boiling water 1-inch deep. Bake at 325° for 1 hour. Cool. Serve with whipped cream.

Delicate cake on top of lemon sauce.

Mae Gay
Brooks, OR

TAPIOCA PUDDING

12 Tbsp. tapioca
8 c. boiling water
1 c. white sugar
1 (3 oz.) box Jell-O
whipped cream
marshmallows and nuts (if desired)
bananas or other fruits

Add the tapioca to boiling water. Cook until clear. Add sugar and Jell-O. Cool, then add your choice of fruit, marshmallows, nuts and the whipped cream.

Strawberries with strawberry Jell-O is very good.

Elsie Kauffman

JELLO TAPIOCA

1 qt. warm water
1 c. sugar
½ c. tapioca
½ c. jello (any flavor)
Cool Whip and fruit

Bring to a boil the warm water, sugar and tapioca. Add the jello. Cool and add Cool Whip and fruit.

Naomi Petersheim
Susie King

LARGE PEARL TAPIOCA

4 c. milk
2 ½ Tbsp. pearl tapioca
⅔ c. sugar
2 eggs
1 tsp. vanilla

Soak tapioca overnight. Cook tapioca in milk until almost clear. Beat eggs. Beat in sugar. Add to milk and tapioca and cook until almost boiling. Add vanilla.

Naomi King

APPLE GOODIE

½ c. sugar
2 Tbsp. flour
¼ tsp. salt
1 tsp. cinnamon
1 ½ qt. apples, sliced

Top Part:

1 c. oatmeal
¾ c. brown sugar
1 c. flour
¼ tsp. soda
⅓ tsp. baking powder
⅔ c. butter

Mix sugar, flour, salt and cinnamon. Add apples and mix. Put on the bottom of a greased pan. Mix the ingredients of Top Part until crumbly, then put on apples and pat firmly. Bake at 350° until brown and crust is formed. Serve with milk or cream.

Fannie Glick

APPLE GRUNT

½ c. sugar (brown)
2 Tbsp. shortening
1 egg
1 c. flour
½ tsp. salt
1 tsp. baking powder
½ tsp. soda
½ c. sour milk or buttermilk
1 ½ c. sliced apples
½ tsp. vanilla

Cream sugar and shortening together and add eggs and beat. Add soda to sour milk and stir into mixture. Sift dry ingredients together and add, beating thoroughly. Add sliced apples and blend into mixture. Pour into greased shallow baking dish.

Crumbs:

6 Tbsp. brown sugar
1 ½ tsp. flour
½ tsp. cinnamon
1 ½ Tbsp. butter

Rub together crumbs. Sprinkle crumbs over top of mixture. Bake at 375° for 35 to 40 minutes. Serve hot with milk.

Rachel King

VANILLA ICE CREAM

1 ½ qt. scalded milk
3 pkg. gelatin
4 c. sugar (scant)
9 eggs
3 cans Carnation milk
1 can condensed milk
6 Tbsp. vanilla

Fill freezer ⅔ full.

Rachel Esh

ICE CREAM
(6 Quarts)

4 qt. rich milk
4 c. sugar (brown or white)
¾ tsp. salt
2 Tbsp. vanilla
2 Tbsp. flour
2 Tbsp. cornstarch
4 eggs, beaten
cream or canned milk may be added

Heat milk, sugar and salt. Mix the flour, cornstarch and eggs with milk enough to make a smooth sauce. Stir into the milk and bring to a boil. Add vanilla and cool.

Mrs. Edna B. Zook

CHOCOLATE SYRUP

4 c. brown sugar
2 c. cocoa
½ c. corn syrup
4 c. white sugar
2 c. water

Mix in a 6 quart kettle until all is blended. Add 2 more cups of water and stir again. Bring to a boil and boil for 5 minutes. (It is very apt to boil over.) Add ¼ cup vanilla. Put boiling hot into jars and seal. Makes approximately 3 quarts.

Linda Fisher

BUTTERSCOTCH TOPPING
(For Ice Cream)

1 c. brown sugar
2 Tbsp. Karo syrup
¼ c. rich milk
3 Tbsp. butter

Combine all ingredients. Stir until boiling and simmer for 3 minutes.

Mrs. Edna B. Zook

CALIFORNIA PUDDING

4 oranges
4 bananas
1 can chunk pineapple
1 c. cream
1 ½ lb. marshmallows

Cook pineapple juice thick with cornstarch and add with cream which has been beaten stiff. Add to the cut up fruits.

Fannie Glick

FANCY RICE PUDDING

½ c. rice
1 Tbsp. cornstarch
3 eggs, separated
1 qt. milk
½ c. sugar
2 Tbsp. margarine
pinch of salt
1 tsp. vanilla

Partially cook rice and drain. Mix egg yolks and cornstarch and a little milk. Add mixture and remaining milk to rice. Add sugar, salt and butter. Cook on top of stove until rice is done. Add vanilla. Pour in baking dish. Top with meringue made of egg whites and brown in oven.

(Vern) Mary Ann Paul

RAISIN PUDDING

Part 1:

2 c. flour
1 c. sugar
2 tsp. baking powder
¼ tsp. salt
1 c. milk

Part 2:

1 c. raisins
2 c. boiling water
1 c. brown sugar
1 Tbsp. butter

Pour Part 1 in greased baking dish. Pour Part 2 on top of dough. Bake at 350° for 35 to 40 minutes.

Edna Zook

BLUEBERRY OR CHERRY PUDDING

2 Tbsp. shortening
2 c. sugar
1 c. milk
2 c. flour
2 tsp. baking powder
2 c. berries
1 c. hot water

Cream shortening and add 1 cup of sugar. Add milk alternately with flour and baking powder and beat smooth. Put batter into greased baking dish. Take another bowl and put berries with the other cup of sugar and 1 cup hot water and stir up good together. Pour that mixture over batter and mix. Bake at 350° for 30 minutes or until done.

(Vern) Mary Ann Paul

DELICIOUS PUDDING

1 Tbsp. vanilla
1 c. brown sugar
¾ c. water
4 Tbsp. butter
1 tsp. salt
½ tsp. soda
¾ c. sugar
6 c. milk
4 eggs
¾ c. flour

Combine first 5 ingredients. When this boils, add soda, milk, egg yolks and flour. Cook until thick.

Priscilla S. King

CARAMEL PUDDING

1 c. brown sugar
4 Tbsp. flour
1 tsp. vanilla
3 egg yolks
½ c. water
1 Tbsp. butter
2 ½ c. milk
12 graham crackers

Melt butter and brown. Add sugar and water and boil. Mix egg yolks, flour and milk. Add to syrup and boil until thick. Add vanilla and put in dish lined with graham crackers and spread on top of pudding. Spread with beaten egg whites and a few graham cracker crumbs and brown slightly.

Elsie Kauffman

CARAMEL PUDDING

6 c. milk, scalded
3 eggs
2 c. brown sugar
3 heaping Tbsp. flour
pinch of salt

Heat milk. In bowl mix eggs, sugar, flour and salt. Beat well. Pour mixture into heated milk, stirring constantly, until thickened. Remove from heat. Add 1 teaspoon vanilla and 2 tablespoons butter. Keep stirring until cool.

Anna Fisher

GRAHAM CRACKER PUDDING

2 pkg. or more graham crackers
2 qt. cornstarch pudding
½ box Cool Whip

Pudding:

2 qt. milk
3 eggs
3 c. sugar
3 heaping Tbsp. flour

Bring milk to a boil. Mix eggs and sugar well. Add flour and add to boiling milk. Stir until thick. Cool. Beat and add Cool Whip.

In a cake pan, put graham crackers (not crumbs) on bottom, then pudding, graham crackers again and pudding. Repeat again and have graham crackers on top. Frost.

Frosting:

3 Tbsp. cocoa
2 tsp. Karo
3 Tbsp. margarine
3 Tbsp. milk
2 Tbsp. oil
2 tsp. vanilla
1 ½ c. 10x sugar

It sets better is it sets a few hours before eating.

Susie King

CORNSTARCH PUDDING

2 qt. milk
3 heaping Tbsp. cornstarch
¾ c. sugar
½ tsp. salt
2 eggs, beaten well
1 tsp. vanilla
½ c. brown sugar

Put all the milk except 1 cup in a saucepan and scald. With remaining cup of milk, add the cornstarch, sugar and salt. Mix, then add the eggs. Stir into milk. Cook until thick. Take off heat and add vanilla and brown sugar.

Aarlanne Petersheim

SWEETHEART PUDDING

1 c. sugar
3 eggs, separated
4 c. milk
7 Tbsp. flour
1 tsp. vanilla

Mix sugar and egg yolks. Add milk, flour and vanilla. Cook to a custard. Pour the custard into crust, then beat egg whites until stiff and pour over custard. Reserve 1 cup crumbs and sprinkle on top. Broil in oven a few minutes.

Crust:

2 c. graham cracker crumbs
⅓ c. sugar
¼ c. margarine

Fannie Riehl

CHEESE CAKE

1 pkg. unflavored gelatin, mix with a little cold water
1 c. sugar
2 egg yolks
1 c. milk
vanilla
8 oz. cream cheese
1 (8 oz.) Cool Whip

Add the sugar and egg yolks to the gelatin and water mixture. Stir and add milk. Cook 2 to 3 minutes. Remove from heat and add vanilla and cream cheese. Cool and add Cool Whip and beaten egg whites. Pour over graham cracker crust.

Naomi Petersheim
Priscilla King

CHEESE CAKE

1 can evaporated milk, chilled
3 oz. lemon jello
1 c. boiling water
30 sq. grahams, crushed
¼ c. melted butter
2 Tbsp. sugar
1 (8 oz.) cream cheese
1 c. sugar
1 tsp. vanilla

Dissolve the jello in the boiling water. Set partly before using. Spread the crushed grahams, melted butter and 2 tablespoons sugar in pan. Save some for top. Bake 10 minutes. Combine cream cheese, 1 cup sugar and vanilla. Beat milk to soft peaks. Add cheese mixture and jello. Pour over crumbs and chill.

Aarianne Petersheim

NO BAKE CHEESE CAKE

1 large box lemon jello
1 (8 oz.) pkg. cream cheese
1 c. sugar
vanilla
1 can Carnation milk

First make jello using only about 3 cups water. Let partly set. Mix cream cheese, sugar and vanilla. Add to jello. Beat Carnation milk and add to jello mixture.

Crumbs:

2 pkg. graham crackers, crushed
¾ stick oleo or butter
2 Tbsp. sugar

Mary Stoltzfus

CHEESE CAKE

2 c. graham cracker crumbs
1 stick butter
1 Tbsp. sugar

Filling:

3 oz. pkg. lemon jello
1 c. hot water
8 oz. pkg. cream cheese
1 can evaporated milk, chilled
1 c. sugar

Whip milk until thick. Combine all ingredients and pour into crust. Put some graham crackers on top.

Elsie Kauffman

CHEESE CAKE

1 pkg. Knox gelatine, dissolved in water
1 c. sugar
1 c. milk
2 eggs
2 (8 oz.) pkg. Philadelphia cream cheese

Put graham cracker crust in bottom of 13 x 9-inch cake pan. Cook gelatine, sugar, milk and eggs together for 2 or 3 minutes. Add a little lemon juice and vanilla. When you add lemon juice to the cooked mixture, it will curl. Soften cream cheese. Add to cooked mixture. Beat egg whites until stiff. Whip 1 cup cream. Mix everything together and pour on top of graham cracker crust. Put in refrigerator.

Fannie Riehl
Sylvia Stoltzfus

CHEESE CAKE

graham crackers
3 oz. pkg. jello
1 (8 oz.) pkg. cream cheese, softened
1 can evaporated milk, chilled
1 c. white sugar

Put grahams in bottom of pan. Dissolve jello in hot water. Beat evaporated milk until fluffy. Add cream cheese. Beat a little and add sugar. Mix jello with the mixture.

Rachel King

PINEAPPLE CHEESE CAKE

9 oz. crushed pineapple, drained
1 pkg. lemon gelatin, make as directed
8 oz. cream cheese
1 c. instant dry milk
1 graham cracker crust

Make jello as directed. Gradually beat gelatin mixture into cream cheese. Chill until thick, but not set. With mixer at high speed, beat in dry milk. Fold in pineapple. Pour into graham cracker crust in a 9 x 9-inch pan. Refrigerate.

Sara Stoltzfus

CHEESE CAKE

2 c. graham cracker crumbs
¼ c. butter or oleo

Mix the graham cracker crumbs with the oleo or margarine. Line bottom and sides of spring-form pan.

Filling:

4 eggs
1 c. sugar
3 pkg. cream cheese
2 tsp. vanilla

Beat eggs well. Gradually add sugar, beating well until it becomes light in color. Add cream cheese in small portions and mix until smooth. Blend in vanilla and turn mixture into crumbs and bake 30 to 40 minutes in a 350° oven.

Helen Miller

CHEESECAKE

Bottom Part:

1 ⅓ c. graham cracker crumbs
⅛ lb. melted butter
1 Tbsp. sugar

Middle Part:

4 eggs
1 ¼ c. sugar
24 oz. cream cheese
1 tsp. vanilla

Top Part:

½ c. sugar
1 pt. sour cream
1 tsp. vanilla

Put crumbs in pan. Pour batter on top. Bake at 350° for 30 minutes. Pour top on and bake 10 to 15 minutes longer.

Naomi King

ICE CREAM DELIGHT

50 Ritz crackers, crushed
¾ stick butter
2 pkg. instant pudding
1 ¼ c. milk
½ gal. vanilla ice cream
½ c. coconut (if desired)
Cool Whip

Line bottom of cake pan with a mixture of crackers and butter. Save ½ cup crumbs for top. Mix pudding and milk. Add ice cream, a little at a time. Coconut may be added. Top with Cool Whip and reserved crumbs and a few cherries.

Susie S. King

ICE CREAM DESSERT

2 pkg. graham crackers (reserve 1 c. for top)
6 to 8 bananas
1 gal. vanilla ice cream
1 c. chocolate chips
2 c. 10x sugar
12 oz. evaporated milk
½ c. butter
1 pt. Cool Whip
1 c. nuts or peanuts

Put graham cracker crumbs on bottom. Slice bananas, then add vanilla ice cream and crushed nuts. Freeze, then melt butter and add chocolate chips. Add milk and 10x sugar. Cook until thick. Cool and put on top of ice cream. Put Cool Whip on, then the rest of crumbs.

Anna King

BLUEBERRY COBBLER

6 tsp. butter, melted
3 c. flour
1 ½ c. milk
2 Tbsp. baking powder
1 ½ c. sugar
1 Tbsp. salt
4 c. blueberries
2 c. sugar
2 ½ c. boiling water
butter

Mix the 6 teaspoons butter, flour, milk, baking powder, 1 ½ cups sugar and salt well and spread in a well buttered large cake pan. Put the blueberries over dough mixture. Put the 2 cups sugar over blueberries. Put the boiling water over blueberries and dot with butter. Bake at 350° for 40 to 45 minutes. After baking, the dough will be on top, the blueberry sauce on the bottom. Delicious hot with cold milk or ice cream.

Katie King
(Hammertown)

PEACH COBBLER

6 to 8 large ripe peaches, sliced
2 ½ Tbsp. cornstarch
1 c. sugar

Crust:

1 c. flour
2 egg yolks
¼ c. butter or oleo melted
1 tsp. baking powder
1 c. sugar
2 egg whites, stiffly beaten

Combine peaches, cornstarch and sugar. Pour into a greased 13 x 9 x 2-inch baking pan.

For Crust: Combine all ingredients except egg whites. Gently fold in egg whites. Spread over peaches. Bake at 375° for 45 minutes.

Mrs. Susie Smucker

PEACH CRUNCH

1 qt. peaches, cut in slices, reserve ¼ c. liquid
12 graham crackers, crushed
1 stick butter, melted
¼ c. brown sugar

Arrange peaches in square baking pan and pour juice over them. Mix grahams, butter and sugar. Sprinkle over peaches. Bake at 350° for 40 minutes.

A handy dessert for unexpected company.

Aarlanne Petersheim

CHERRY COBBLER DESSERT

¼ c. shortening
1 c. sugar
1 egg
1 ½ c. flour
½ tsp. salt
2 tsp. baking powder
1 Tbsp. tapioca
1 Tbsp. lemon juice
2 Tbsp. butter
⅓ c. milk
2 c. cherries

Sift flour, baking powder, salt and sugar together. Cut shortening in dry ingredients. Beat egg. Add milk. Combine with flour mixture. Pour cherries into greased pan. Sprinkle with tapioca, lemon juice and butter. Drop batter in 6 mounds on top of cherries. Bake at 400° for 30 minutes.

Mrs. Edna B. Zook

PEACH COBBLER

1 egg, beaten
1 c. granulated sugar
butter, walnut size
2 c. flour
1 tsp. baking powder
½ tsp. vanilla
little salt
½ c. milk

Place fruit in bottom of baking dish. Follow with a little brown sugar and flour on top. Pour batter over fruit. Bake at 375° for about 1 hour.

Liz Stoltzfus

RHUBARB CUSTARD

2 c. rhubarb
1 c. granulated sugar
1 Tbsp. flour
2 eggs
1 c. milk
1 Tbsp. butter

Mix rhubarb, sugar and flour. Put into a greased baking dish. Beat eggs. Add milk. Pour this over the rhubarb mixture. Sprinkle with a bit of cinnamon and put butter on top. Bake for 10 minutes at 425°, then turn oven down to 350° and bake about 15 or 20 minutes more.

Rachel King

CUSTARD PUDDING

1 qt. milk
1 c. white sugar
2 Tbsp. flour
2 Tbsp. cornstarch
2 eggs
pinch of salt
vanilla

Put graham cracker crumbs in casserole first, then put pudding in last. Beat egg whites last.

Rachel King

A RECIPE FOR REST

When at night you sleepless lie
and the weary hours drag by,
Lift your thought to God above
bending down to you in love.
Feel his presence by your bed
His soft touch upon your head
Let your last thought be a prayer,
as you nestle in his care
Ask Him all your way to keep
then O, then drop off to sleep.

BERRIED DELIGHT

1 (8 oz.) pkg. cream cheese
¼ c. sugar
2 Tbsp. milk
1 ½ c. Cool Whip
2 (4 serving size) pkg. vanilla instant pudding
3 ½ c. milk

Beat the cream cheese, sugar and milk. Fold in Cool Whip. Spread over graham cracker crust. Top with desired fruit. Prepare pudding with the milk. Pour over berries. Chill overnight or several hours. Delicious with blueberries.

Nancy Ann Esch
Elizabeth Stoltzfus

FINGER JELLO

4 envelopes unflavored gelatin
4 pkg. flavored gelatin (3 oz. each)
6 c. boiling water

Combine flavored and unflavored gelatin in a bowl. Add boiling water. Pour into a layer pan and refrigerate. When firm, cut into squares.

Sylvia Petersheim

ORANGE FLUFF JELLO SALAD

1 medium can crushed pineapple
⅓ c. sugar
1 large pkg. orange jello
9 oz. Cool Whip
1 small can mandarin oranges

Cook pineapple (don't drain) and sugar together 10 minutes. Cool in refrigerator. Dissolve jello in 1 ½ cups boiling water. Refrigerate until it starts to jell. Beat gelatin mixture with electric mixer until fluffy. Stir in cooled drained pineapple until well mixed. Fold in Cool Whip.

Sylvia Petersheim

LEMON DESSERT

½ c. margarine
1 c. flour
½ c. nuts

Mix and bake until brown. Cool.

Center:

1 c. 10x sugar
1 c. Cool Whip
8 oz. cream cheese

Mix and put on crust.
Mix lemon as directed on box for topping or a can of lemon pie filling.

Naomi King
Susie King

JOLLY JELLO

1 pkg. raspberry jello (3 oz.)
1 pkg. orange jello (3 oz.)
2 pkg. lime jello (6 oz.)
1 pkg. Dream Whip, prepared as directed on box

Separately dissolve 1 package of each flavor jello with 1 ½ cups boiling water each. Pour into pans. Let set until firm. Dissolve remaining lime jello into 1 ¼ cups boiling water. Chill until syrupy. Beat well with beater. Fold Dream Whip into beaten jello and cut firm jello in pieces and fold in.

Sylvia Petersheim

PINEAPPLE SNOW

- 1 pkg. orange gelatin
- 1 c. hot water
- 1 c. pineapple juice and remaining water
- ½ c. sugar
- 1 c. crushed pineapple, drained
- ½ c. whipping cream

Dissolve gelatin in hot water. Add pineapple juice and remaining water. Chill until partially congealed. Whip until fluffy. Add drained pineapple. Whip the whipping cream and add sugar.

Anna King

TAPIOCA JELLO

- ½ c. pearl tapioca
- 5 c. boiling water
- 1 c. sugar
- 3 oz. orange jello
- 1 pkg. whipped topping

Put tapioca in boiling water. Let set overnight. Cook until clear, about 7 to 10 minutes. Add sugar and jello. When ready to serve, add 1 package whipped topping. Add oranges, if preferred.

Mary Stoltzfus

PEACH EMERALD DELIGHT

- 1 box peach jello (large)
- 2 (8 oz.) cream cheese
- 2 c. Cool Whip
- 1 can mandarin oranges

Add 2 cups water with jello. Mix soft cream cheese and ½ cup sugar together. Gradually add to jello. Put in fridge to thicken. Add oranges and Cool Whip.

Susie S. King

CHRISTMAS SALAD

1st Layer:

3 ½ c. hot water
¾ c. lime jello
1 can pineapple, drain and save juice

Let stand 4 to 6 hours.

2nd Layer:

1 c. pineapple juice
1 ½ tsp. gelatin, dissolved
3 oz. cream cheese
1 pkg. Dream Whip

Cook the pineapple juice and add the dissolved gelatin. Remove and add the cream cheese. Chill, then add the Dream Whip.

3rd Layer:

3 ½ c. boiling water
¾ c. strawberry jello

Aarianne Petersheim
Mrs. Elam Z. Stoltzfus

FROZEN PUMPKIN DESSERT

1 ½ c. graham cracker crumbs
¼ c. sugar
¼ c. butter or margarine, melted
1 (16 oz.) can pumpkin
½ c. brown sugar
½ tsp. salt
1 tsp. ground cinnamon
¼ tsp. ground ginger
⅛ tsp. ground cloves
1 qt. vanilla ice cream, soften
whipped cream
toasted coconut

Mix crumbs with sugar and butter. Press into bottom of a 9-inch square pan. Combine pumpkin with brown sugar, salt and spices. Fold in ice cream. Pour into crumb lined pan. Cover and freeze until firm. Take out of freezer about 20 minutes before serving and top with whipped cream and toasted coconut.

Priscilla King

ORANGE DESSERT

1 qt. water
½ c. clear jell
1 pkg. orange Kool-Aid
1 ¼ c. sugar

Bring these to a boil. Cool. Add grapes, pineapple and peaches. Just before serving, add a few bananas.

Barbara King

APPLE DESSERT

¾ c. rolled oats
¾ c. brown sugar
½ c. flour
½ c. oleo
pinch of salt
1 tsp. cinnamon

Mix together. Spread over apples in a square pan or pie pan. Bake at 350° for 40 minutes.

Barbara Zook

RHUBARB DESSERT

1 ½ c. sugar
2 Tbsp. clear jell
½ c. water
4 c. diced rhubarb

Combine and cook.

Crumbs:

1 c. brown sugar
1 ½ c. flour
1 c. uncooked oatmeal
1 c. melted butter
sprinkle with cinnamon

Press half of crumbs in bottom of pan and rhubarb, then rest of crumbs.

Barbie Zook
Rachel Esh

RHUBARB CREAM DELIGHT

Crust:

1 ½ c. flour
3 Tbsp. sugar
¾ c. butter or margarine

Cream Filling:

2 c. sugar
4 egg yolks, beaten
⅔ c. cream or evaporated milk
3 Tbsp. flour
½ tsp. nutmeg
4 c. chopped rhubarb

Meringue:

4 egg whites
¼ c. sugar

Combine crust ingredients until crumbly. Press into a 13 x 9 x 2-inch baking pan. Bake at 350° for 20 minutes. While crust is baking, combine all filling ingredients and cook in heavy saucepan over medium heat. Stir constantly until thickened. Watch carefully because mixture will scorch easily. Pour hot filling onto crust. Top with meringue made by beating egg whites with sugar until thick and satiny. Bake at 325° for 15 to 20 minutes or until brown.

Ruth Stoltzfus

WHOLESOME RHUBARB CRUNCH

1 c. whole wheat flour
¾ c. uncooked oatmeal
¾ c. brown sugar
½ c. melted butter
1 tsp. cinnamon

Mix until crumbly. Press half of crumbs in bottom of a 9-inch baking pan. Cover with 4 cups diced rhubarb.

1 c. sugar
2 Tbsp. cornstarch
1 c. water
1 tsp. vanilla

Combine and cook until thick and clear. Pour over rhubarb. Top with remaining crumbs. Bake at 350° for 1 hour.

Elizabeth Stoltzfus

RICE KRISPIE DESSERT

¼ c. corn syrup
2 Tbsp. firmly packed brown sugar
3 Tbsp. butter
2 ½ c. Rice Krispies
¼ c. peanut butter
¼ c. Hershey's syrup
3 Tbsp. corn syrup

Mix the ¼ cup corn syrup, brown sugar and butter and cook on low heat until it boils. Add the Rice Krispies and press mixture into a 9-inch pie pan. Mix together the peanut butter, Hershey's syrup and 3 tablespoons corn syrup and spread on crust. Place in freezer until hard. Fill with 1 quart soft vanilla or chocolate ice cream. Let stand at room temperature for 10 minutes before serving.

Liz Stoltzfus

DANISH DESSERT

1 ½ Tbsp. cornstarch or clear jell
⅓ c. sugar
pinch of salt
¼ c. jello (any flavor)

Heat to boiling 1 cup water or juice. Combine jello, sugar and cornstarch. Make a paste with ½ cup juice. Stir in boiling juice and stir until thick and clear. Pour over fruit.

Naomi Grace Zook
Sylvia Stoltzfus
Barbie Zook

JELLO SALAD

1 (6 oz.) box jello
1 (8 oz.) cream cheese
1 ¾ c. boiling water
¾ c. cold water
1 (8 oz.) container Cool Whip

Mix cream cheese and jello. Add water. Beat in Cool Whip. Refrigerate several hours.

Mary Ann Smucker

JELLO DESSERT

1 pkg. jello
1 envelope Dream Whip
1 can fruit cocktail (16 oz.)

Make jello and Dream Whip according to directions. Cool jello until set. Add rest of ingredients and chill 3 hours.

Barbie Zook

JELLO DESSERT

2 (9 oz.) boxes Cool Whip
3 c. cottage cheese
2 small boxes orange-pineapple jello
1 can crushed pineapple
1 can mandarin oranges

Mix the Cool Whip, cottage cheese and jello together and add the pineapple and oranges.

Fannie Riehl

INDIANA SALAD

1 c. lime jello
4 c. boiling water
1 large can crushed pineapple, drained
nuts (if desired)
1 c. whipped cream
1 (8 oz.) pkg. Philadelphia cream cheese
juice from pineapple
¾ c. sugar
3 level Tbsp. flour
3 egg yolks
pinch of salt

First Part: Mix jello. When starting to set, add pineapple and nuts.

Second Part: Mix together whipped cream and cream cheese. Mix until smooth and put on First Part when set.

Third Part: To the juice of the pineapple, add sugar, then add enough water to juice to make 1 ½ cups. Stir flour up with water. Add eggs and salt. Cook until smooth and cool and put on top.

Aarianne Petersheim
Naomi Grace Zook
Anna King
Sylvia Stoltzfus
Naomi Petersheim

MILLIE'S ICE CREAM DELIGHT

50 Ritz crackers, crushed
¾ stick butter
2 pkg. instant vanilla pudding
1 ¼ c. milk
½ gal. vanilla ice cream
½ c. coconut
Cool Whip
cherries

Line bottom of pan with crackers mixed with butter. Save ½ cup crumbs for top. Mix the pudding and milk. Add the ice cream a little at a time. Coconut can be added. Top with Cool Whip, crumbs and a few cherries.

Susie King

PEARL JELLO TAPIOCA

½ c. pearl tapioca
5 c. boiling water
1 c. sugar
3 oz. orange jello
1 pkg. whipped topping
oranges

Mix the tapioca and boiling water and set overnight. Next morning cook until clear, about 7 to 10 minutes. Add the sugar and jello. When ready to serve, add the whipped topping and oranges.

Barbara King

YUM YUM SALAD

1 (20 oz.) can crushed pineapple
1 pineapple can water
½ c. sugar
1 (6 oz.) box strawberry Jell-O
2 pkg. whipped topping mix
8 oz. pkg. cream cheese

Boil crushed pineapple, water and ½ cup sugar for 5 minutes. Turn burner off and add Jell-O. Cool. Mix whipped topping mix with milk and add cream cheese and beat. Mix to first part. Just use spoon to beat together.

Barbara King
Mary Stoltzfus
Edna B. Zook

OREO COOKIE DESSERT

Oreo cookies, crushed
Cool Whip
1 c. 10x sugar
8 oz. pkg. cream cheese
3 c. milk
instant vanilla pudding
instant chocolate pudding

First Layer: Mix crushed cookies and 6 tablespoons melted butter well and put in a pan.

Second Layer: Mix well 1 cup Cool Whip and 1 cup 10x sugar and the cream cheese.

Third Layer: Mix 1 package vanilla pudding and 1 package chocolate pudding with 3 cups milk. Top with Cool Whip and sprinkle with cookie crumbs.

Ruth Stoltzfus
Liz Stoltzfus

CREAM PUFF DESSERT

Crust:

1 c. water
1 stick butter
1 c. flour
4 eggs

Put water and butter in saucepan and bring to a boil. Take off stove and add flour all at once. (Cool.) Add eggs one at a time, beating well after each addition. Spread into a greased and floured 13 x 9-inch pan. Bake at 400° for 30 minutes. Cool.

Filling:

2 small boxes instant vanilla pudding
3 c. milk
1 (8 oz.) cream cheese
1 (8 oz.) container Cool Whip

Beat the pudding, milk and cream cheese well and pour over cooked crust. Top with Cool Whip and drizzle with chocolate syrup or icing.

Mary Ann Smucker

APPLE CRISP

6 large apples
1 c. flour
½ c. brown sugar
¼ lb. butter
2 Tbsp. white sugar
¼ tsp. cinnamon

Grease a deep glass baking dish. Put in sliced apples. Mix together with sugar and cinnamon. Sprinkle over apples. Mix flour, brown sugar and butter. Pour over apples. Bake at 400° for 35 to 40 minutes.

Ruth Stoltzfus

APPLE GOODIE

½ c. sugar
2 Tbsp. flour
¼ tsp. salt
1 tsp. cinnamon
1 ½ qt. apples, sliced

Top Part:

1 c. oatmeal
¾ c. brown sugar
1 c. flour
¼ tsp. soda
⅓ tsp. baking powder
⅔ c. butter

Mix sugar, flour, salt and cinnamon. Add apples and mix. Put on the bottom of a greased pan. Mix ingredients of Top Part until crumbly, then put on apples and pat firmly. Bake at 350° until brown and crust is formed. Serve with milk or cream.

Sylvia Stoltzfus

OLD-FASHIONED APPLE DUMPLINGS

6 medium size baking apples
2 c. flour
2 ½ tsp. baking powder
½ tsp. salt
⅔ c. shortening
½ c. milk

Sauce:

2 c. brown sugar
2 c. water
¼ c. butter

Pare and core apples. Leave whole. Sift flour, baking powder and salt. Put in shortening and mix like pie crumbs. Sprinkle milk over mixture and make into a dough. Roll dough and cut into 6 squares. Place an apple on each. Fill cavity in apple with brown sugar and cinnamon. Put dough over apple to cover it completely. Put dumplings in greased baking pan. Cook sauce for 5 minutes and pour over dumplings. Bake 35 to 40 minutes at 375°.

Mary Stoltzfus

ECLAIRS

1 c. water
½ c. butter
1 c. flour
4 beaten eggs

Boil water and butter, then add flour and eggs. Put by tablespoon on greased cookie sheets. Bake at 350° for 30 to 40 minutes.

Icing:

⅓ c. chocolate chips
1 c. 10x sugar
1 tsp. corn syrup
¼ c. evaporated milk
1 tsp. vanilla

Melt chocolate chips and milk, then add rest of ingredients.

Eclair Pudding:

1 ⅓ c. sugar
10 Tbsp. flour
4 c. milk
½ tsp. salt
4 eggs, beaten
2 tsp. vanilla

Combine sugar, flour and salt in a pan. Slowly stir in milk. Place over heat. Bring to a boil, stirring constantly. Remove from heat. Stir in a little of this mixture into eggs. Pour back into hot mixture. Bring to a boil, then add vanilla.

Fannie Glick

ECLAIR DESSERT

6 c. milk, heat
6 egg yolks
3 heaping Tbsp. flour
3 heaping Tbsp. cornstarch
1 ½ c. sugar
½ c. brown sugar
1 (8 oz.) box Cool Whip

Mix the milk, egg yolks, flour, cornstarch, sugar and brown sugar together. When cool, add the Cool Whip. Lay grahams in bottom of pan. Put half of pudding on and crackers on top again. Add rest of pudding on top. Add grahams on top and put icing on.

Icing:

3 Tbsp. cocoa
2 Tbsp. oil
2 tsp. cornstarch
2 tsp. vanilla
3 Tbsp. butter or margarine, soft
3 Tbsp. milk
1 ½ c. 10x sugar

Put on grahams as soon as icing comes to a boil.

Rachel King

FRUIT PIZZA

Crust:

2 c. flour
2 sticks butter
2 Tbsp. sugar

Press on pizza pan. Prick with fork. Bake at 350° for 15 minutes or until golden brown.

Filling:

1 large bowl Cool Whip
2 (8 oz.) pkg. cream cheese
¾ c. 10x sugar
2 Tbsp. milk

Spread on cooled crust and top with fresh fruit.

Ruth Stoltzfus

LEMON JELLO

2 large pkg. lemon jello
8 large marshmallows
1 c. crushed pineapple, drained
2 bananas, sliced

Melt marshmallows in hot jello. (Let cool.) Add pineapple and sliced bananas before jello sets.

Topping:

1 egg, beaten
1 c. pineapple juice
½ c. sugar
2 Tbsp. butter
2 Tbsp. flour
1 pkg. Dream Whip

Cook the egg, pineapple juice, sugar, butter and flour until thick. (Cool.) Mix the Dream Whip according to directions. Fold in topping mixture. Spread on jello. Sprinkle ½ cup crushed nuts on top.

Katie S. King

-• EXTRA RECIPES •-

Ways in Which Sugar Affects Texture of Foods

In cakes, used in right proportions, sugar helps to make them tender and light. Too much sugar makes cake tough and heavy.

In breads, used in right proportions, sugar helps to make them light. Too much sugar makes bread coarse in texture.

With fruit juices, used in right proportions, makes fruit juice jelly. Too much sugar makes jelly "wine off" and makes it soft and sticky in texture. Too little sugar necessitates over-cooking, impairs flavor and gives a tough texture.

In beaten egg white, sugar helps the egg to hold air and remain stiff. Too much sugar makes the egg whites flatten out and settle.

Beverages, Microwave & Miscellaneous

When some people get into a jam they shake like jelly.

A Prayer

"Give me good digestion, Lord,
And also something to digest,
Give me a healthy body, Lord,
And sense to keep it at its best,
Give me a healthy mind, good Lord,
To keep the good and pure in sight,
Which, seeing sin is not appalled
But finds a way to set it right.
Give me a mind that is not bound,
That does not whimper, whine or sigh.
Don't let me worry over much
About the fussy thing called I.
Give me a sense of humor, Lord,
Give me the grace to see a joke,
To get some happiness from life,
And pass it on to other folk."

Patience is accepting a difficult situation without giving God a deadline to remove it.

BEVERAGES, MICROWAVE & MISCELLANEOUS

ICE CREAM PUNCH

1 qt. orange
2 qt. water
2 qt. ginger ale
1 qt. vanilla ice cream

Mix all ingredients together and chill.

Katie King
(Hammertown)

WEDDING PUNCH

2 ½ c. pineapple juice, chilled
1 pt. lime, lemon or raspberry sherbet
1 pt. vanilla ice cream
1 (12 oz.) bottle ginger ale or 7-Up

Combine pineapple juice, sherbet and ½ of ice cream. Beat until smooth. Add 7-Up or ginger ale. Spoon remaining ice cream into punch. Serve immediately.

Susie King

LEMONADE

6 lemons
1 ½ c. sugar
2 ½ qt. water

Slice lemons in thin rings. Add sugar and pound to extract juice. Let stand 20 minutes and then add cold water and ice cubes. Stir until well blended. Makes 3 quarts.

Linda Fisher

HAM SALAD SANDWICHES

2 c. ground, cooked ham
3 stalks celery
1 large dill pickle
¼ tsp. dry mustard
¼ tsp. onion powder
½ c. mayonnaise
½ tsp. salt
1 Tbsp. lemon juice

Put ham, celery and pickle through coarse blade of food chopper. Add remaining ingredients and mix.

Edna Zook

GRILLED SALMON SANDWICHES

1 (8 oz.) can red or pink salmon, well drained
⅓ c. finely chopped celery
2 Tbsp. sweet pickle relish, well drained
⅛ tsp. ground pepper
¼ c. mayonnaise
8 slices bread

Mix all ingredients except bread and spread on 4 slices of bread. Top with remaining bread slices and brown on griddle.

Linda Fisher

CARAMEL POPCORN

8 qt. popcorn, popped
2 c. brown sugar
2 sticks butter
½ c. molasses
1 tsp. salt
½ tsp. soda
a little vanilla

Melt butter. Add brown sugar, soda and molasses, then pour over popcorn and mix well. Put on two trays or cookie sheet and bake at 250° for 1 hour. Stir every 15 minutes while baking.

Naomi King

CARAMEL POPCORN

1 c. butter
2 c. brown sugar
½ c. molasses
1 tsp. salt
½ tsp. soda
1 tsp. vanilla
7 qt. popcorn

Cook the butter, brown sugar, molasses and salt for 5 minutes. Time as soon as sugar is melted. Add the soda and vanilla. Pour over popcorn. Put on cookie sheet. Bake at 250° for 30 minutes. Stir often.

Fannie Riehl
Rachel Esh
Priscilla King

HOMEMADE SHAKE 'N BAKE

1 c. flour
2 Tbsp. paprika
dash of pepper
2 Tbsp. seasoned salt
1 tsp. baking powder

Mix and pour into plastic bag. Wet chicken to coat. Coats 4 or 5 pieces.

Aarianne Petersheim

GRANDMA

She lets him go barefoot in the summertime
And swing on the garden gate.
She lets him eat cookies between meals
And stay up disgracefully late.
She indulges him when he visits
She was stricter with her boy.
But this one isn't hers to raise,
Only to enjoy!

GRAPE JUICE

grapes
4 c. juice
1 c. sugar

Use as many grapes as you want to cover with water. Set on stove and boil 10 minutes. Strain and return to kettle. Measure 4 cups juice. Boil the juice and sugar together 4 minutes. Put in jar and seal.

(Vern) Mary Ann Paul

CANNED APPLE PIE FILLING

4 ½ c. white sugar
1 c. cornstarch
2 tsp. cinnamon
2 tsp. lemon juice
1 tsp. salt
10 c. water
few drops yellow food coloring

Blend first 3 ingredients in large saucepan. Add salt. Stir in water. Cook and stir until boiling. Add lemon juice and food coloring. Take off heat. Slice apples in quart jars. Pour hot sauce over top. Cold pack 20 minutes. Makes enough sauce for 7 quarts of apples.

Katie King
(Hammertown)

CANNED MEATBALLS

15 lb. ground beef
½ c. salt
4 slices bread
36 Premium crackers
1 c. oatmeal
3 c. water or more
4 eggs

Mix well. Butcher will grind it with ground beef, if you wish. Pack in jars. Boil 3 hours.

Susie S. King

CORNED BEEF

50 lb. beef (roasts, steaks or any choice cut)
3 qt. salt

Place meat in large crock or other suitable container and add salt alternately. Let stand overnight, then rinse off roughly and pack in crock again.

Brine:

¼ lb. baking soda
¼ lb. saltpetre
2 lb. brown sugar
2 Tbsp. liquid smoke
enough water to cover meat well

This meat will be ready for use in 2 weeks. It can be canned (cold pack 3 hours) or put in freezer. If crock is kept in a cool place, meat may be kept in brine up to 3 months.

Rachel Esh

PIZZA SAUCE

10 qt. tomato juice
4 c. sugar
4 Tbsp. salt
4 Tbsp. oregano
1 Tbsp. chili
1 Tbsp. garlic powder
⅓ c. salad oil

Cook 30 minutes, then thicken with clear jell. Put in jars while cooking. No need to cold pack. (This is a mild sauce.)

Katie King
(Hammertown)

PIZZA SAUCE

2 gal. tomato juice
1 Tbsp. oregano
1 Tbsp. garlic powder
1 Tbsp. black pepper
½ Tbsp. red pepper
1 box pickling spice
1 qt. vinegar
6 c. sugar

Boil together 1 hour, then put through strainer and back in kettle. Bring to boil. Thicken with clear jell, at least 3 cups. Put in jars.

Fannie Glick

PIZZA SAUCE

6 c. tomato juice
1 ½ c. Ragu spaghetti sauce
1 Tbsp. brown sugar
½ c. chopped onion
1 tsp. salt
2 tsp. garlic
¾ tsp. oregano

Bring to a boil and thicken with ½ cup clear jell. Fill 9 (1 cup) jars. Cold pack 30 minutes.

Fannie Riehl

PIZZA SAUCE

3 qt. tomato juice
1 c. brown sugar
1 tsp. salt
¾ tsp. black pepper
1 tsp. garlic salt
1 tsp. oregano
1 tsp. chili powder
2 Tbsp. vegetable oil
2 c. onions, chopped
1 c. peppers, chopped

Brown onions and peppers in oil and add the remaining ingredients. Bring to a boil and simmer for 20 minutes. Thicken with clear jell. Cold pack for 30 minutes.

Edna B. Zook
Anna King
Barbara King
Anna Fisher
Linda Fisher

SPAGHETTI SAUCE

½ bushel tomatoes
2 garlic onions
3 green peppers
1 hot pepper
3 lb. onions
1 pt. oil
1 ½ or 2 c. sugar
½ c. salt
1 tsp. basil
1 Tbsp. oregano
8 small cans tomato paste or just thicken with clear jell

Cook tomatoes, garlic and onions together, then strain. Cut peppers in the pint of oil. Cook until soft enough to put through strainer. Add to juice, then add the rest of the ingredients and cook until thick. Put in jars and seal.

Rachel Esh

SPAGHETTI SAUCE

6 onions, chopped
2 peppers, chopped
6 qt. tomato juice
6 c. catsup
6 tsp. oregano
2 tsp. garlic powder
6 tsp. salt
3 tsp. pepper
sugar to taste

Brown onions and peppers in ¼ cup vegetable oil. Combine all ingredients and simmer until desired thickness. This can be frozen or canned.

Naomi King

CATSUP

8 qt. tomato juice
8 c. granulated sugar
1 tsp. red pepper
1 tsp. black pepper
3 c. vinegar
2 Tbsp. salt
small box ground mustard

Cook tomato juice 1 hour. Add other ingredients and cook for another hour. Pour into bottle and seal.

Anna Fisher
Linda Fisher

CATSUP

3 qt. tomato juice
3 Tbsp. dry mustard
a little pepper
small tsp. salt
¼ tsp. chili powder
3 drops oil of cloves
3 drops oil of cinnamon
1 pt. vinegar
1 ½ qt. sugar

Cook until thick (about 3 hours).

Sylvia Stoltzfus

KETCHUP

2 gal. tomato juice
1 pt. vinegar
1 qt. sugar
1 tsp. ginger
2 tsp. cinnamon
½ tsp. cloves
½ tsp. pepper
1 tsp. nutmeg
4 tsp. salt

Cook until thick enough to suit, about 3 to 4 hours.

Mary Stoltzfus

CATSUP

8 qt. tomato juice
2 qt. granulated sugar
1 tsp. red pepper
1 tsp. black pepper
2 Tbsp. salt
1 ½ pt. vinegar

Cook all ingredients 1 ½ hours. Add 1 small box ground mustard. Continue cooking until thick enough.

Ruth Stoltzfus

KETCHUP

4 qt. tomato juice
3 red peppers
4 onions
2 Tbsp. salt
3 c. sugar
½ c. vinegar
2 tsp. celery salt
2 tsp. mustard
½ tsp. allspice
½ tsp. cloves
1 tsp. cinnamon
1 tsp. paprika

Combine tomatoes, peppers, onions, sugar and spices. Cook 1 hour. Add vinegar and cook until thick.

Naomi Petersheim

PEPPER AND CABBAGE SLAW

1 c. sugar
1 c. water
3 Tbsp. vinegar

Grind cabbage through a food chopper. Dice peppers real fine. Mix and put in jars. Cook water mixture to dissolve sugar. This is enough for 1 quart. Cold pack 20 minutes. This recipe is good for small stuffing peppers, too.

Mary Stoltzfus

SWEET PEPPERS

peppers
½ pt. vinegar
3 c. water
3 c. sugar
1 tsp. vegetable oil
1 tsp. salt

Clean and cut peppers and pack in jars. Mix together the remaining ingredients and boil. Pour over peppers and cold pack 10 minutes.

Aarianne Petersheim

SAUERKRAUT

cabbage
salt

Shred cabbage and pack into jars. Add 1 teaspoon salt to each quart and fill with boiling water. Seal tightly. Do not cold pack. Place jars on tray or newspaper as some juice may run out.

Aarianne Petersheim

CANNED CANTALOUPE

2 c. water
5 c. sugar
2 c. vinegar
½ Tbsp. salt

Heat together. Makes enough for about 6 quart jars. Cold pack 30 minutes.

P.S. One tablespoon alum may be added to syrup to keep lopes firm.

Nancy Ann Esch

PICKLED CANTALOUPE

10 c. sugar
3 pt. water
2 c. vinegar

Bring to a boil. Use firm cantaloupe. Cut in dices and put in jars. Pour brine in jars. Cold pack 5 to 10 minutes.

Anna Fisher

TO CAN RED BEETS

¾ c. vinegar
¼ c. water
¼ tsp. salt
1 c. sugar

Cook red beets until soft. Take skin off. Slice in quarters and pack in jars. Heat vinegar, water, salt and sugar until almost boiling. When sugar is dissolved, pour over beets in jars and seal. Cold pack for 15 to 20 minutes. The juice used to cook the beets may be used instead of water. Makes enough brine for 1 quart beets.

Sara Stoltzfus

TO CAN PEPPERS

peppers
vegetable oil
salt

Cut peppers in strips and pack into jars. Add 1 teaspoon vegetable oil and 1 teaspoon salt to each quart jar.

Syrup:

2 c. vinegar
3 c. water
3 c. sugar

Mix, then pour over peppers while boiling hot. Seal. Cold pack until the boiling point.

Linda Fisher

FREEZE CORN

4 qt. cut corn
1 c. sugar
2 c. water
4 tsp. salt

Boil 15 minutes on simmer. Cool and freeze.

Susie S. King
Fannie Riehl
Anna Fisher

A MOTHER'S PRAYER

Oh, give me patience when wee hands
Tug at me with their small demands.
And give me gentle and smiling eyes
Keep my lips from hasty replies.
And let not weariness, confusion or noise
Obscure my vision of life's fleeting joys.
So when in years to come,
My house is still
No bitter memories its room may fill.

RED BEET JELLY

6 c. beet juice
½ c. lemon juice
2 boxes Sure-Jell
8 c. sugar
1 (6 oz.) pkg. jello (raspberry or strawberry)

Combine first 3 ingredients and bring to a hard boil. Add sugar and jello and boil 6 to 8 minutes longer.

Naomi Grace Zook

PEACH MARMALADE

5 c. crushed peaches
1 small can crushed pineapple
7 c. sugar
2 small or 1 large box peach jello

Cook the peaches, pineapple and sugar 20 minutes. Add the jello. Stir until jello is dissolved, then put in jelly jars.

(Hammertown)
Katie King
Barbara King

DANDELION JELLY

1 qt. blossoms, without stems
1 qt. water
1 box Sure-Jell
1 tsp. lemon or orange extract
4 ½ c. sugar

Its taste resembles honey. In the early morning pick the blossoms without the stems. Boil blossoms with water for 3 minutes. Drain off 3 cups liquid and add the Sure-Jell, lemon or orange extract and sugar. Boil about 3 minutes.

Rachel Esh

UNCOOKED FREEZER JAM

4 c. strawberries, crushed to 2 c.
1 pkg. Jel-ease fruit pectin
4 c. sugar

Wash, stem and crush berries thoroughly. Place in 4 quart kettle. Gradually stir sugar into fruit and let stand 10 minutes. In a separate small saucepan mix pectin with ¾ cup water. Bring to a boil, stirring constantly and boil hard for 1 minute. Immediately stir pectin mixture into fruit and continue stirring for 3 minutes. Fill jars. Cover and let stand at room temperature for 24 hours. Store jam in freezer. After thawing, jam will keep in refrigerator about 3 weeks. Makes about 4 ½ cups.

Sylvia Stoltzfus

PEACH JELLY

5 c. mashed peaches
7 c. sugar
1 can crushed pineapple
2 (3 oz.) boxes orange or peach jello

Bring the peaches, sugar and pineapple to a boil and boil for 15 minutes. Add the jello. Stir and pour into jars and seal.

Barbie King
Elizabeth Stoltzfus
Katie King
(Hammertown)

APRICOT JELLY

2 c. apricots
1 c. apples
1 c. water
3 ½ c. sugar
¼ tsp. alum

Bring to a boil water, apples and apricots. Add sugar and alum and boil 20 minutes.

Rachel Esh

ZUCCHINI JELLY

6 c. grated zucchini
6 c. granulated sugar
½ c. lemon juice
6 oz. crushed pineapple with all the juice
6 oz. apricot jello or your favorite flavor

Boil the zucchini 6 minutes or until clear, then add the sugar, lemon juice and pineapple with all the juice. Boil 6 minutes, stirring constantly. Remove from heat and add the jello. Cold pack 10 minutes.

Priscilla King

OLD FASHIONED JELLY

5 lb. sugar
1 gal. white Karo
2 qt. strawberries or whatever you're using

Cook for 20 minutes and jar. Gives a good sticky jelly.

Priscilla King

RHUBARB JELLY

4 c. finely cut rhubarb
4 c. sugar
1 c. water
1 can crushed pineapple
1 (3 oz.) box strawberry jello

Combine first 3 ingredients and let stand 3 hours, stirring occasionally. Bring to a boil and boil 10 minutes. Add pineapple and boil again for 7 minutes. Remove from heat and add jello.

Rachel Esh

RHUBARB JAM

5 c. rhubarb, cut fine
4 c. sugar
1 small pkg. strawberry jello

Let the rhubarb and sugar stand overnight. In the morning, boil 5 minutes, then add the jello. Boil 3 minutes.

Edna Zook

BLACK RASPBERRY JAM

3 qt. raspberries
4 c. juice
1 pkg. Jel-ease fruit pectin
5 ½ c. sugar

Wash, crush and simmer about 5 minutes, covered. Squeeze out juice through cloth or bag. Put juice into 6 or 8 quart saucepan. Stir Jel-ease into juice. Place on heat and stir continuously while bringing to a full boil. Gradually add the sugar, stirring well to dissolve it.

Bring to a full rolling boil that cannot be stirred down, stirring constantly. Start timing and continue boiling for 2 minutes. Remove pan from heat and fill hot jars to about ¼-inch from the top.

Sylvia Stoltzfus

PINEAPPLE JELLY

1 ½ lb. sugar
5 lb. white Karo syrup
1 qt. crushed pineapple

Cook 20 minutes only or it will get too stiff.

Susie S. King

SANDWICH SPREAD

6 red peppers
6 green peppers
6 green tomatoes
6 pickles, unpared (green)
6 onions (medium size)
2 c. vinegar
4 c. sugar
1 c. flour
½ pt. mustard

Cut vegetables in pieces or strips. Put salt on these and let stand 2 hours. Drain, then grind in food grinder. Add the vinegar, flour and sugar. Cook 15 minutes. Add the mustard and cook 5 minutes more, stirring constantly, as it burns easily. Put in jars and cold pack 5 to 10 minutes.

(Hammertown)
Katie King

APPLE BUTTER

1 gal. applesauce
6 c. sugar
2 c. cider
8 tsp. cinnamon
1 tsp. cloves

Cook slowly for 3 hours.

Fannie Riehl

APPLE BUTTER
(Oven Method)

7 lb. apples (16 c.)
3 lb. brown sugar
1 c. vinegar or cider
2 Tbsp. cinnamon

THE GAME

Anne detested washing dishes, which was her daily chore
And each time she did it, she just disliked it more.
She claimed, "There is no other job, that I much more dislike."
This mournful speech her mother heard, where she rocked baby Mike.

"Why, Anne! What makes you hate it so? Your grumbling makes me sad.
If you would want to like it, it wouldn't be so bad."
"But I don't want to like it," said Anne, decision made.
"I'm sure I'd rather do your work, I'd gladly with you trade."

"Now Anne, you know I am your Mom, and children must obey.
I want to tell you something, now, you want to hear - okay?
Washing the dishes can be fun, if you want it to be
And you can make it be a game, that's fun to play, you see?

You get the cups and wash them all, then next come forks and knives.
When those are washed and cleaned you do, the spoons by fours and fives."
"The bowls and plates are next in line, the kettles you do last,
Then all at once you realize the dishes got done fast!"

"You make it sound so easy, Mom," said Anne with widened eyes,
"But maybe I could try it, then, I might have a surprise!"
The next day when the time to wash, the dinner dishes came
Anne barely could wait long enough, to try out Mother's game.

So gladly at the job she went, to like it was her aim–
The very-much-detested task, had turned into a game!
How glad Anne's Mother was about, her daughter's victory,
And so her Mother-heart rejoiced the wondrous change to see.

D. Stauffer

INDEX OF RECIPES

Meats & Main Dishes

Vegetables

Breads, Rolls & Pastries

INDEX OF RECIPES

Cakes, Cookies & Desserts

Beverages, Microwave & Miscellaneous

Be A Good Conversationalist

Help the other party get started talking by asking questions about things or places he is interested in. A good conversationalist listens much more than he talks. Practically everyone likes to talk about the things he is interested in.

A good conversationalist rarely misses the opportunity to give a sincere compliment or well deserved praise and this is sure to enhance you in his opinion. (Caution: Do not give undeserved praise as this is apt to cause exactly the opposite effect as desired and your listener may think you are being sarcastic.)

When in a group do not single out any one person, try to get the whole gathering discussing the same thing. This helps the timid soul and keeps the party from becoming trying and uninteresting.

It is poor taste to make witticisms at the expense of another. Never try to be the life of the party by telling stories about someone else unless the incident is something he would like to hear and be proud of. If you want to provoke a laugh, let the joke be on yourself.

The following examples are good and bad points toward helping you to be a good mixer:

DO BE	DON'T BE
1. A swell informed as possible	1. A bore
2. Broad-minded	2. Die-hard
3. Original	3. Gossip
4. Enthusiastic	4. Boaster
5. Considerate	5. A mental absentee
6. Interesting	6. Windbag
7. Dramatic	7. Wise-cracker
8. Attentive	8. Boisterous
9. Unselfish	9. Single-tracker
10. Able to let the other person talk as much as possible.	10. Interrupter

Making children's beanbags? Save peach and plum seeds and cherry pits, wash and dry them, and fill the bags. They are lightweight and easy to use.

Bee Stings

An 1840 antidote for bee stings: "Bind on the place a thick plaster (paste) of saleratus (soda bicarbonate) moistened; it will soon expend the venom."

Burns

Many different things will help the pain of burns: cold water, milk and egg white; a thin paste of bicarbonate of soda in cold milk or vinegar; cold witch hazel extract; honey; vanilla extract; a thin slice of potato.

Headaches

Why use drugs that could be dangerous? Do place a cold compress of witch hazel over forehead. A white-coated tongue often indicates that your headache is caused by an upset stomach. Try some sage tea made by steeping a leaf in water for a few minutes.

Insect Bites

Dissolve a heaping teaspoonful of sodium bicarbonate in vinegar and use with an equal part of cold witch hazel. Or saturate a piece of cotton with household ammonia and press it on the sting for a few minutes.

Poison Ivy

Make a thick solution of brown washing soap in hot water. Apply as warm as possible every hour for 4 or 5 hours. If you know you have been exposed to poison ivy, take the immediate precaution of washing the exposed area with this brown soap. Most likely, you will thereby prevent a serious rash.

Flowers

Cut flowers last longer if the leaves below the water level are removed. Also, the water will stay fresher.

To make your cut flowers last longer, place them in a solution of tea, diluted 1 part tea to 4-6 parts water.

To prevent colorful flowers from fading for weeks, cut the stems off about 3/4 inch and let them stand in a weak solution of glycerin, one teaspoon to 7-8 ounces of water.

Preparing a flower arrangement? Omit sweet peas. They have a devastating, wilting effect on other flowers.

A novel effect: Add a few drops of food coloring to your clear glass flower bowls. To make the stems appear less conspicuous, add a few drops of green food coloring.

Cornstarch

A generation ago, cornstarch served young mothers as a dusting powder to absorb the child's excessive skin secretions; and grandmothers cleaned their furs by gently rubbing a little in with gentle pressure and shaking the fur thoroughly.

Cough Remedy

Need a cough remedy in a hurry? Mix 2 teaspoons of lemon juice in 1/2 to 2/3 cup of warm water and add enough honey to thicken. Take 1 or 2 teaspoonfuls every hour as needed.

Aloe

Aloe is a nice houseplant, easy to care for. If you keep a plant on your sill, you have on hand a remedy for chapped hands, insect bites, sunburn scalds. Press the gummy juice from the leaves for this medicine. For bad burns, a jelly-like substance will hold better to the skin. Prepare this with a solution of tea and Irish moss, then add the gummy juice of the aloe.

Aluminum Foil

If you need a trivet for a hot pot, wrap some foil around several thicknesses of newspaper. Not unattractive!

Shaped foil makes a good emergency funnel.

Be very careful when you use aluminum foil near your electric stove. Although it appears in sheets, this metal product is a good conductor, which can give you the shock of your life if it makes contact with any exposed electrical element of your kitchen.

Emergency Substitutions

1 Tbsp. cornstarch = 2 Tbsp. flour or 4 tsp. tapioca (for thickening)

1 tsp. baking powder = 1/4 tsp. baking soda plus 1/2 c. buttermilk or sour milk (to replace 1/2 c. liquid called for in recipe)

1 cake compressed yeast = 1 pkg. or 2 tsp. active dry yeast

1 c. sour milk or buttermilk = 1 Tbsp. lemon juice or vinegar plus sweet milk to make 1 c. (let stand 5 minutes)

1 whole egg = 2 egg yolks (in custards)

1 sq. unsweetened chocolate = 3 Tbsp. cocoa plus 1 Tbsp. butter or margarine

1 Tbsp. fresh snipped herbs = 1 tsp. dry herbs

1 small fresh onion = 1 Tbsp. instant minced onion, rehydrated

1 tsp. dry mustard = 1 Tbsp. prepared mustard

1 clove garlic = 1/8 tsp. garlic powder

1 c. tomato juice = 1/2 c. tomato sauce plus 1/2 c. water

1 c. catsup or chili sauce = 1 c. tomato sauce plus 1/2 c. sugar and 2 Tbsp. vinegar (for use in cooked mixtures)

Happy Homemaker's Secrets

To make your glasses sparkle add a little laundry bluing to your dish water.

To prevent lumpy gravy add a little salt to the flour before adding the water.

To cool a dish of hot food quickly, set it in a pan of cold water which has been well salted.

To prevent broken china when washing dishes place a thick folded cloth in the bottom of the pan.

When using butter, remember that one stick (a quarter of a pound) is equal to 1/2 cup when measured.

When inserting curtain rods in curtains, place a thimble over end of rod.

To prevent hot fat from splattering, sprinkle a little salt, or flour, in it before frying.

Baked beets are more delicious when prepared the same as baked potatoes. They have a sweeter and better taste than when they are boiled.

Instead of greasing a pancake griddle, rub it with a cut raw potato when hot and it will not sick or have an unpleasant odor.

To avoid shelling fresh peas, wash them carefully and cook them as they are. When done the pods will rise to the surface and can easily be skimmed off, which adds to the flavor.

To remove pin feathers easily, take turkey out of oven at the end of the first thirty minutes of roasting and remove with tweezers.

Put lemons in hot water for several minutes before squeezing and they will yield more juice.

To prevent the juices from a berry pie from running over in the oven, stick a few short pieces of large macaroni through the center of the top crust.

To remove odor from the pan after frying fish fill pan with vinegar and let come to a boil.

Eggs can be prevented from spreading while poaching if the boiling water is stirred in one direction and the egg is dropped in the middle of the swirl.

Add a few cloves to vegetable soup to give it a delicious flavor.

To stop nuts and fruits from sinking to the bottom of cakes, heat the nuts, etc., in the oven and then mix in a little flour before adding to the batter.

Brooms will last longer if you dip them once a week in a pail of boiling suds. This makes them tougher and more pliable.

Percolator coffee-stained? Then use a cup of salt, percolate as for coffee, and it will be bright as new.

Bread flour may often be used instead of cake flour. Seven-eighths cup of bread flour plus two tablespoons of cornstarch is equivalent to one cup of cake flour.

Grease cup before measuring molasses, then it will not stick.

To keep egg yolks for several days, cover with cold water or place in an air-tight jar, then store in a cool place.

To measure 1/4 cup of fat, fill cup 3/4 full of cold water, then a add enough fat to bring water to the top of the cup. Any fraction of a cup can be measured in the same way.

Rhubarb substitute for apple sauce in your favorite applesauce cake recipe makes a delicious cake.

Marshmallows placed on top of cup cakes before thoroughly baked adds a delightful flavor, also marshmallows used on open faced pie instead of meringue is good.

Use wet or buttered scissors when cutting marshmallows and dates into small pieces.

After cooking onions, rub an apple over the stove and it will counteract the onion odor.

Add cinnamon or any good spice to your regular waffle recipe for a Sunday evening supper.

When soup is too salty, put in a pinch of brown sugar. This will overcome the salty taste and still not sweeten it.

Clean straw hats by washing with soap and water, then with oxalic acid.

To sharpen scissors, cut through fine sandpaper.

To cream butter, place in a warm bowl, using a wooden spoon and rubbing against side of bowl until soft. Do not melt.

Do not scrape burnt toast with a knife, rub across a grater.

To remove string easily from string beans, put in boiling water for five minutes after washing them.

To remove a fish bone from the throat, cut a lemon in two and suck the juice of it slowly. This softens the bone and will give instant relief.

To remove rust from sink, use a soft cloth dipped in kerosene. Use vinegar to remove rust stains from leaky faucets. Rinse and rub dry.

Use kerosene to remove finger marks on woodwork.

To keep the ice cube tray from sticking, the tray must be dry on outside then place rubber fruit jar rings under tray.

Sniffing lemon juice into the nostrils will cure a nose bleed.

In decorating ice cubes: Any food coloring may be used in coloring cubes. Red cherries or fresh mint leaves frozen in tray make an attractive cube for lemonade.

Freeze 1/2 tray full of water and freeze. Place cherry or fancy cut lemons in each section, cover with a thin layer of water and allow to freeze.

For grape juice cubes, pour the juice into ice tray and freeze about 3 hours.

For ginger ale cubes pour ginger ale into ice tray and freeze about 3 hours.

To prevent milk from curdling, add a little salt.

When making pudding or creams, add a pinch of baking soda and it will prevent the milk from curdling.

To prevent frosting from breaking when cut, add a teaspoon of vinegar.

Bread should never be wrapped in cloth, as the cloth absorbs the moisture and gives it an unpleasant taste.

To warm over biscuits or rolls and keep them soft, place them in a pan and place the pan in another pan with hot water.

In cooking vegetables, uncover all those which grow above the ground and cook covered all those which grow under the ground.

For cleaning piano keys use a piece of muslin dipped into alcohol. For very yellow keys, use cologne water.

To remove grease, oil, etc., from wallpaper apply clean absorbent paper over area stained and iron with hot iron–change paper until spot is removed.

For tomato stain, soak stained part in sour milk, then wash.

Silks may be cleaned with potato juice. Get two large potatoes and grate them into a pint of water, this proportion applying to the amount you desire to use. Let the potato starch settle to the bottom, then pour out the clear liquid and bottle it. Lay silk upon a board, apply the potato juice with a sponge until it is clean. Rinse in cold water. Gasoline may also be used, but should be used cautiously.

Anytime you need some sour cream which you don't have, make an imitation of it by putting a tablespoon of vinegar with a cupful of evaporated milk.

You can prevent fresh frosting from running off the top and down the sides of a cake by dusting flour across the cake as soon as the frosting is put on. Not enough to alter the taste of the icing but just enough to make it congeal.

To prevent a salad from getting soggy, put a saucer upside down in the bottom of the bowl first, then put the salad on top of it.

Keep brown sugar in a large jar with dried prunes. The prunes keep the sugar from turning hard, the sugar sweetens the prunes.

Marbles can be used as a safety alarm to let you know when the pot is running dry. The marbles, when the water gets low, will make a fearful racket.

Favorite Recipes

Recipe Name	**Page No.**

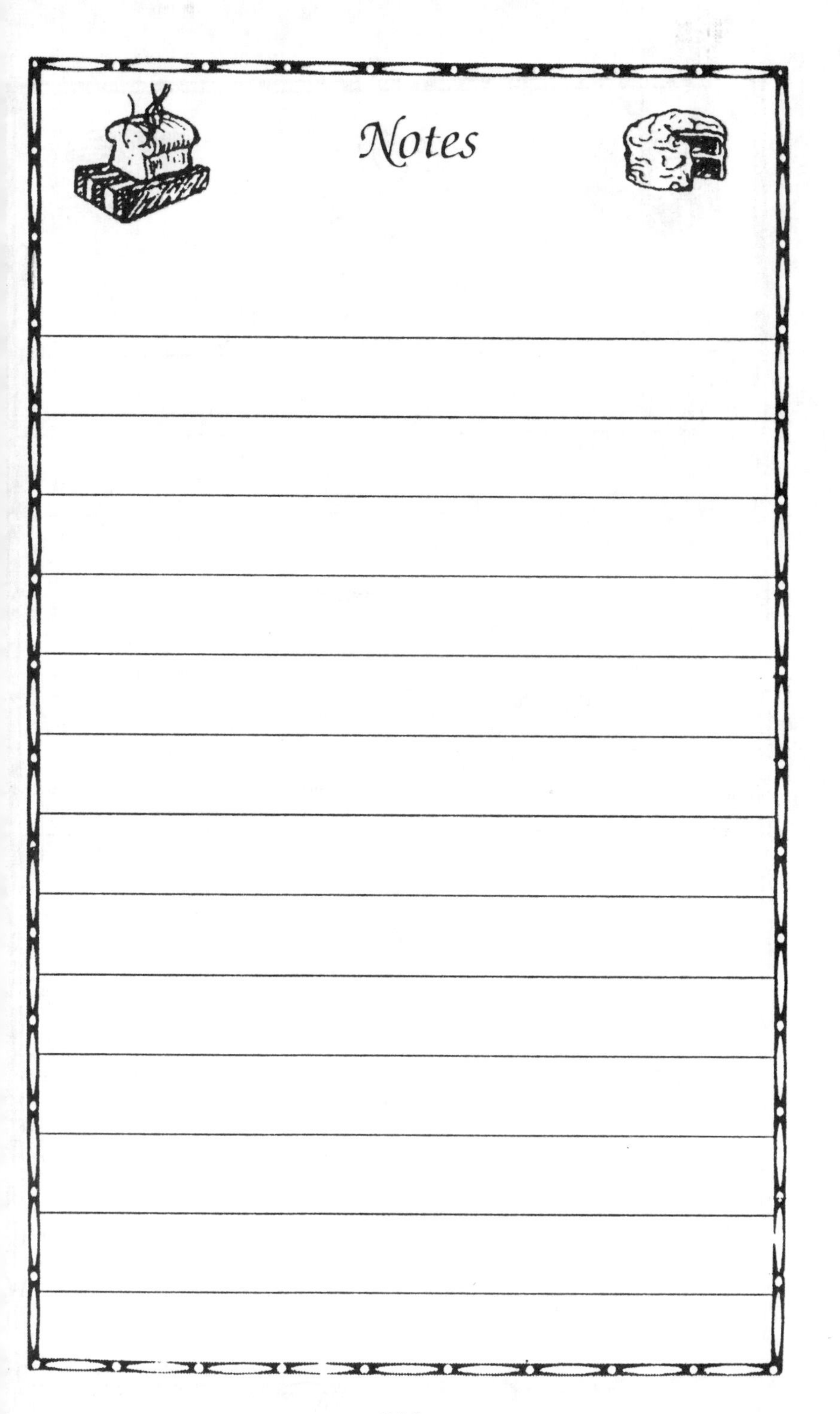
Notes

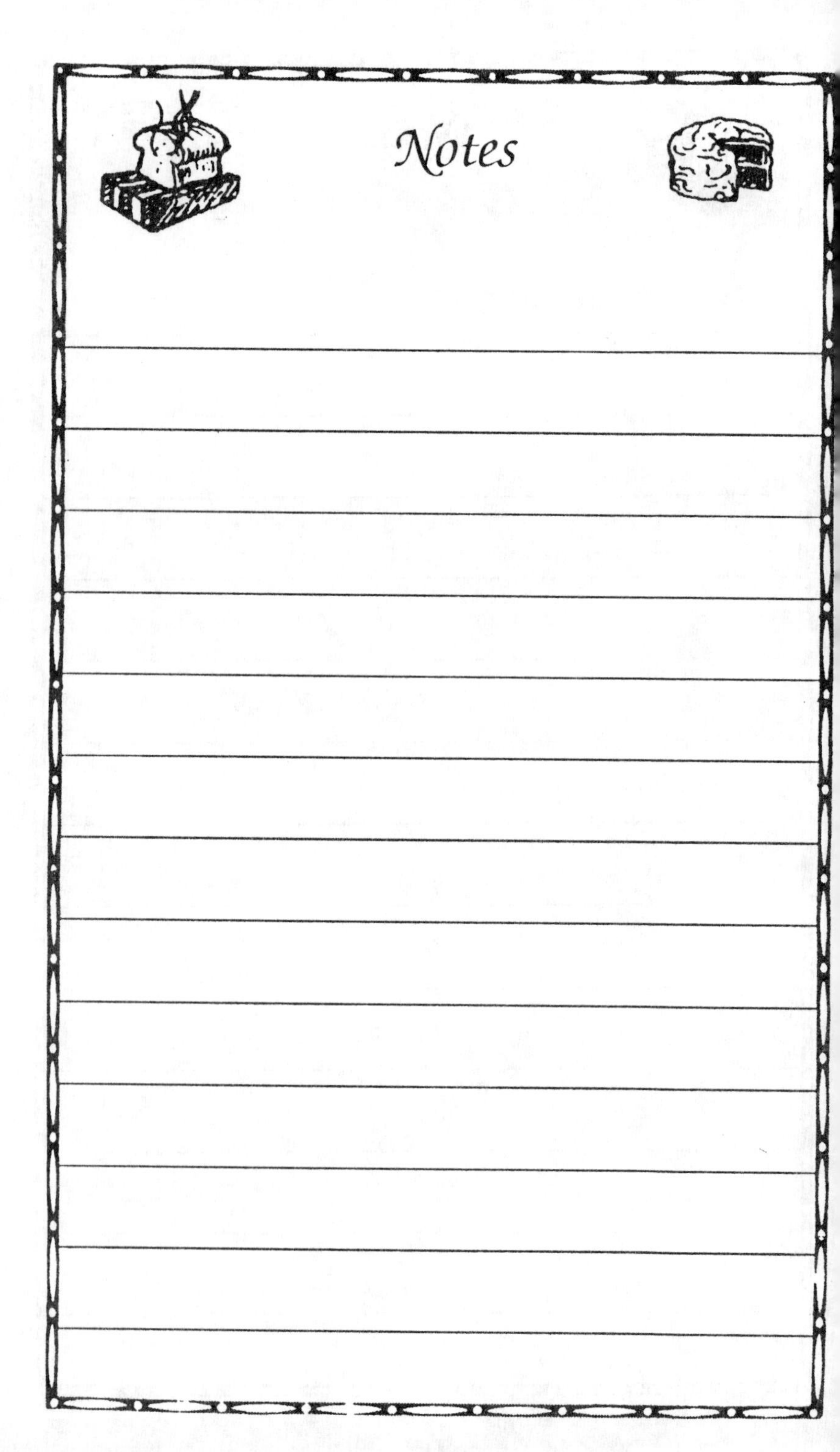
Notes

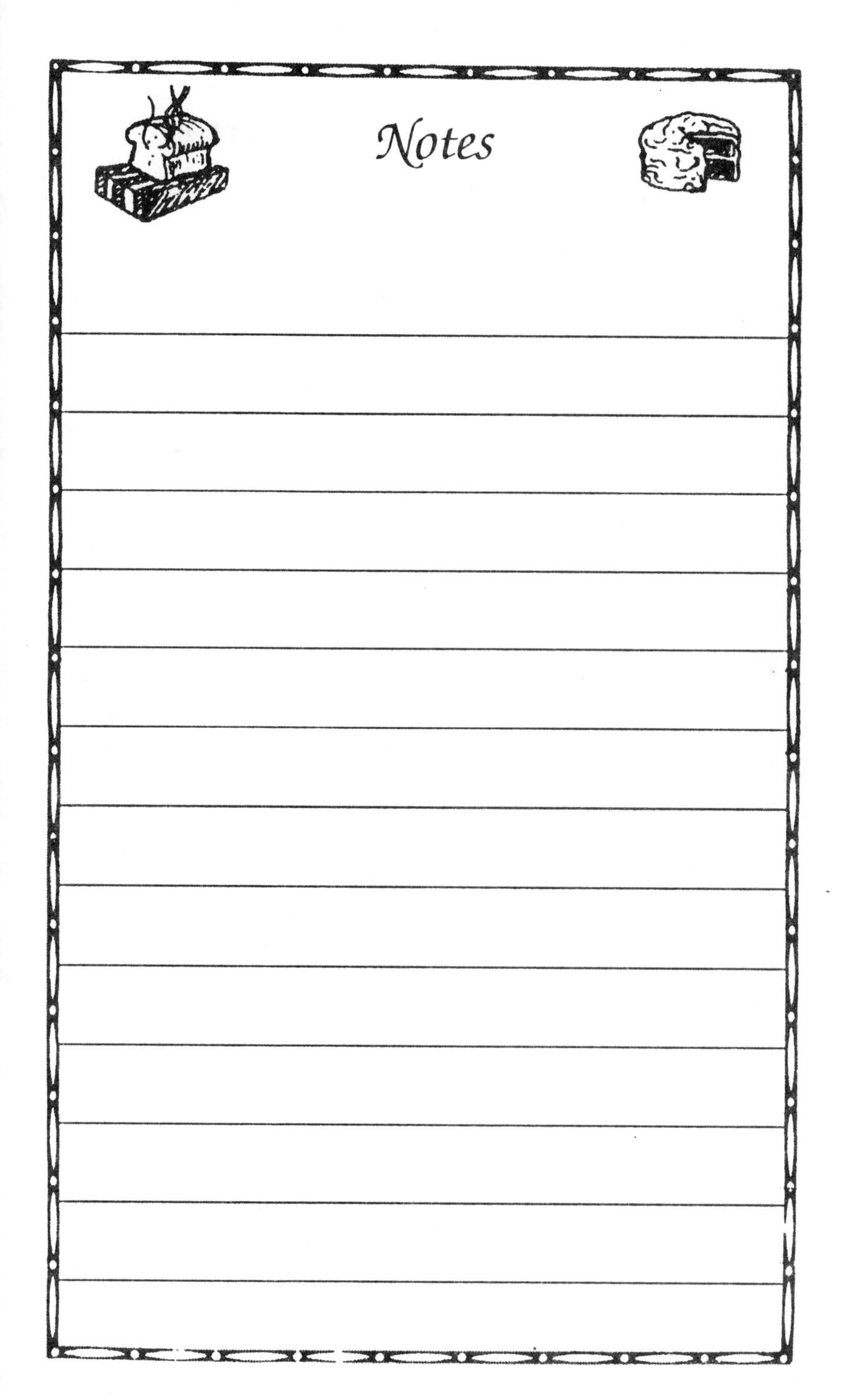
Notes